Make My Life An Adventure

Devotions for Women — Adventures of a Christian Mother

Jeanette Stohlmann

Illustrations by

Ken Hiller

Wisconsin Evangelical
Lutheran Synod
(605) 352-9947
for more information

Scripture taken from the
HOLY BIBLE, NEW INTERNATIONAL VERSION
Copyright © 1973, 1978, 1984 International Bible Society
Used by permission of Zondervan Bible Publishers.

All rights reserved. Except for brief quotations in critical articles or reviews, no part of this book may be reproduced in any manner without prior permission from the publisher.

Library of Congress Card 90-62387
Northwestern Publishing House
1250 N. 113th St., Milwaukee, WI 53226-3210
© 1990 by Northwestern Publishing House
Printed in the United States of America
ISBN 0-8100-0357-0

DEDICATED TO:

My loving husband, Steve, and our precious children:

Naomi Christine
Seth Patrick Christian
Mary Elizabeth
Micah Stephen
Philip James

Contents

God Is with You	1
Doxology	3
We Will See Jesus	5
Therefore Go	7
Walking and Leaping and Praising God	9
Bread Baking in the Oven	11
Constant Love	13
Praying about Little Things	15
My Purpose in Life	17
Leave It in the Lord's Hands	19
The Way Home	21
A Quiet Place	23
Cocoa on My Bible	25
Running the Race with Patience	27
Loving My Teenager	29
Always Under the Umbrella	31
Yes, No, Wait	33
Lists, Lists, Lists	35
More than Enough	39
Praise God at All Times	41
Not Just a Spectator	45
Like a Little Child	47
Free! Free Indeed!	49
Fear Knots and Fear Nots	51
The Most Satisfying Work	53
Really Clean	55
The Little Things Mean So Much	59
Let Your Light Shine	61
A Lesson on Hands	63
Joy to the World	65
Resting in God	67

The Praise Cake	69
The Laughter Chapter	71
Speak to One Another with Psalms	75
Trust Level	77
Jesus Loves You, Mommy	79
The Worry List	81
Fitting into God's Plan	83
His Mercy Endures Forever	87
His Eye Is on the Sparrow	89
The Best Part	91
My Dream	93
Overflowing with Praise!	95
With God All Things Are Possible	97
The Good Guy Always Wins	99
Airmail to Heaven	101
Circling Things in the Christmas Catalog	103
The Secret of Contentment	105
The Lost Sheep	107
The Open Heart	109
My Pet Projects	111
Opposite Day	113
Perfect Peace	115
The Importance of Warm Fuzzies	117
Living on the Mountain Top	121
Evelyn's Shining Light	125
God's Mighty Acts	127
Pray About Everything	129
Motivation for Prayer	133
The Wonderful Winter Wonderland	135
Things that Go "Bump in the Night"	137

FOREWORD

One of the blessings of children attending a Lutheran school is memory work. One wintry morning one of my five children came bouncing into my bedroon and exclaimed, "Mom, time to get up!" Blurry-eyed I sat up in bed. "Mom", he continued, "What's Philippians 4:4?"

I thought for a moment. "Is it,'Rejoice in the Lord always, and again I say, Rejoice'?"

"Right!" he announced happily and bounded off.

"What a nice thought to start the day!" I mused.

"Rejoice in the Lord always!" is the *essence* of this book.

It is my prayer that God will use this book to lead many people to rejoice in the Lord in all situations. God is good. He showers us daily with many blessings. His love is constant. With the Holy Spirit's help, we can rejoice in the Lord always. May the Lord make your life a beautiful ALLELUIA for him!

Ephesians 3:20,21

> Now to him who is able to do immeasurably more than all we ask or imagine, according to his power that is at work within us, to him be glory in the church and in Christ Jesus throughout all generations, forever and ever! Amen.

I would like to thank my husband and children for allowing me the time to write this book. I would also like to express my thanks to Janice Retzlaff and Phyllis Boettcher for the fine job they did typing my manuscript. Finally, I would like to thank my parents, Clarence and Dorothy Zabel, who provided me a model for rejoicing in the Lord.

To God alone be glory!
Jeanette Dorothy Stohlmann

Make My Life an Alleluia!

God Is with You

Joshua 1:9
*Have I not commanded you? Be strong and courageous. Do not be terrified; do not be discouraged, for the L*ORD *your God will be with you wherever you go.*

These words echoed in my ears as my mother read them the night before I took off from the Rochester, Minnesota airport for Adelaide, Australia. The unknown and the far away stretched before me. I was in my early twenties and on my way to teach in a Lutheran school half way around the world. I wondered if the airplane would arrive there safely, and what my future would be like there.

God certainly was with me in the year I spent in Australia. He protected me numerous times in dangerous situations—crossing narrow bridges and riding my bike through heavy traffic, to mention some. The night before I took the plane back home, I almost drowned in the ocean off the coast of Adelaide. The tide took me out, and I could no longer feel my feet on the ocean floor. Being a poor swimmer, I called out to the people hosting the farewell party for me on the shore, but they could not hear me. God helped me use my arms to push back the water and fight my way back to the shore.

Sometimes being in a new situation and living in a new place can be lonely and frightening. A friend of mine and her family of four small children moved to our town from a city five hundred miles away. Their former home had not been sold, so they could barely afford renting their new place, since her husband was attending the seminary. My friend felt lonely and forgotten in their new location. Together we prayed that they would be able to sell their house and that they would know God's constant and abiding presence even in rough times. Gradually things began to improve. My friend joined the church choir and ladies' groups and made many new friends. Her whole outlook brightened, and their former house was sold.

Moses encouraged Joshua in Deuteronomy 31:8: "The Lord himself goes before you and will be with you; he will never leave you nor forsake you. Do not be afraid; do not be discouraged."

Prayer:
Dear Jesus, you have promised to be with me always. Help me to be strong, courageous and bold, knowing that you walk beside me wherever I go. Thank you, Jesus, for being near at all times to share my joys and sorrows, and to preserve my body and soul until we meet face to face. Amen.

Doxology

Romans 11:33-36
Oh, the depth of the riches of the wisdom and knowledge of God! How unsearchable his judgments, and his paths beyond tracing out! "Who has known the mind of the Lord? Or who has been his counselor?" "Who has ever given to God, that God should repay him?" For from him and through him and to him are all things. To him be the glory forever! Amen!

I tell people I met my husband on my front doorstep. They never tire of hearing about our unusual whirlwind romance. I met my husband through letter writing, suggested by my sister and her husband (a seminary colleague of my husband). She noticed from my letters that I was going through a lonely period, trying to adjust to teaching in Adelaide, Australia, just as Steve, a big city boy, was suffering from loneliness as a single pastor in rural Nebraska!

I agreed to write to him and to trust that this Steve was not too terribly ugly. When I received my first letter from Steve, I smiled the whole afternoon. My third graders could not figure out why Miss Zabel was so radiantly happy. The letter was very clever and very funny. It made me laugh and yet it was sensitively and intelligently written. Maybe I was laughing because, after four years of college and two years of teaching, I was convinced that all the good guys were taken. And then there was Steve. What a surprise! Daily we sent letters, tapes and photos back and forth through the mail. The postmaster in the rural Hampton, Nebraska post office was beginning to surmise that the preacher was in love.

On my birthday Steve sent a huge bouquet of beautiful flowers F.T.D. all the way to Adelaide. Enclosed was a note that won my heart: "All my love, Steve." Although we had never met, we knew we liked each other a lot. In fact Steve loved me with a faithful and persistent fervor that I had never before experienced.

He proposed to me through a letter, and on December 17, 1974, we met on the doorstep of my childhood home on a farm in Plainview, Minnesota. He introduced himself and we shook hands. I said, "Oh, that's what you look like." (He is actually nice looking—Ha!) We were engaged that very night and married a month and a half later at Immanuel Lutheran Church, Plainview, Minnesota.

After many unsuccessful years of searching for the right mate, God literally handpicked someone just right for me in a way so unexpected and unbelievable that I am still amazed. God is faithful in answering our prayers, and his paths are "beyond tracing out!" Steve and I have not only found an abundance of joy, happiness and security in each other, but also much joy and wonder in the gifts of five healthy children. God's blessings throughout our courtship and married life have been innumerable. "For from him and through him and to him are all things. To him be the glory forever! Amen!"

Prayer:

I praise you, O God. To you alone belongs all the praise and glory now and forever! You sustain my life and fill it with good things. You renew my strength and lift me up as on wings of an eagle. You satisfy me with your constant love and care. Take my dreams, God, and in your own timing fulfill them to your praise and glory. Amen.

We Will See Jesus

John 14:1-3
Do not let your hearts be troubled. Trust in God; trust also in me. In my Father's house are many rooms; if it were not so, I would have told you. I am going there to prepare a place for you. And if I go and prepare a place for you, I will come back and take you to be with me that you also may be where I am.

When my little seven-year-old daughter, Mary, had her five baby teeth pulled for orthodontic purposes, she had to be put under general anesthetic. As Mary and I entered the doctor's office, we saw a little girl recovering from her operation. She was holding her Dad's hand and whimpering, "When I woke up, I was scared." The nurse explained that it was common to experience an emotional release following the general anesthetic.

Mary's teeth extraction only took a few minutes,

and the nurse came into the waiting room to tell me that Mary was ready to see me. Mary slowly opened her eyes. "Were you scared when you woke up?" I asked.

"No," she replied sweetly, "because I saw you."

When we die, what a comfort it will be to wake up and see Jesus. There will be no fear, only the loving face of our Lord. Yet even Christians wonder if they will go to heaven. We wonder if we will be accepted. But Jesus assures us in John 6:47, "I tell you the truth, he who believes *has* everlasting life." So eternal life is something we already possess through Jesus' death for our sins and his victorious resurrection. When we die we don't have to be afraid, because we will wake up and see Jesus.

Prayer:
Lord God, be with me and tenderly assure me of complete forgiveness of my sins through Jesus' death and the shedding of his holy, precious blood. Keep me on the path that leads to eternal life. In Jesus' name. Amen.

Therefore Go

Matthew 28:19
"Therefore go and make disciples of all nations, baptizing them in the name of the Father and of the Son and of the Holy Spirit."

I had talked with him about the weather, the traffic, the children getting so tall, his childhood, his wonderful garden, and once in a while about church. He was the old man across the street, a widower and overweight, drowning his sorrows in drinking. He had belonged to a church once, but that was a long time ago. I knew my time was running out to tell him about Jesus before he died. I prayed, "Lord, send your Holy Spirit to guide him."

Then I wrote him a note about how God loves him all the time and accepts him because of Jesus' death and resurrection. I attached the note to a vase of three red roses. Since he was not home, I left it inside the screen door. About an hour later I heard a knock at my door. It was my neighbor, beaming with smiles and thanking me profusely for the note and flowers. As we talked I couldn't help but wonder if the joyful message of the gospel had broken through to him by the overwhelming power of the Holy Spirit.

I still witness to my neighbor and thank God for the little gaps in our conversations when I can tell him of God's care for him. Recently he was severely sick, and God provided him with renewed health and strength. The change was so dramatic that my neighbor confessed it was God who had healed him.

Prayer is an important part of witnessing because then we know that we never go into a situation alone. "Therefore go" means not only into all the world, but right across the street.

Prayer:
Lord, thank you for the many opportunities you give me to witness for you through deeds of love and through words. Prepare the way before I talk to someone about you. Send your Holy Spirit to guide me and the other person. I praise you, Lord, for all you do for me and through me. Amen.

Walking and Leaping and Praising God!

Acts 3:1-8
One day Peter and John were going up to the temple at the time of prayer at three in the afternoon. Now a man crippled from birth was being carried to the temple gate called Beautiful, where he was put every day to beg from those going into the temple courts. When he saw Peter and John about to enter, he asked them for money. Peter looked straight at him, as did John. Then Peter said, "Look at us!" So the man gave them his attention, expecting to get something from them. Then Peter said, "Silver or gold I do not have, but what I have I give you. In the name of Jesus Christ of Nazareth, walk." Taking him by the right hand, he helped him up, and instantly the man's feet and ankles became strong. He jumped to his feet and began to walk. Then he went with them into the temple courts, walking and jumping, and praising God.

It had been a rough day. I barely had time to eat. I had been packing boxes for our move to Canada. The Ryder Rental lady arrived with more packing boxes. The phone rang frequently. Three of my children had friends over to play. There was a quick trip to the grocery store for soda and goodies to entertain the kids, a trip to piano lessons, and a trip to the dentist. I ate breakfast at 4:00 p.m. At night I bathed the younger children and made up their beds. Yes, it was a hectic day. It was one of those days when life goes at such a fast clip that it seems there is little quiet time for prayer.

Feeling "blue," I was collapsing in a kitchen chair when my seven-year-old walked in singing a lively song with the chorus:

> He went walking and leaping and praising God!
> Walking and leaping and praising God!
> In the name of Jesus Christ
> Of Nazareth, rise up and walk!

Immediately my sagging spirits lifted. The words "praising God" caught my attention. I praised God for getting me through the day.

Later that night my husband walked in with some great news. My husband taught a college adult learning class, Christian Faith, as part of a total program to grant degrees to people in the community within a shortened time span. That evening one of the women who had fallen away from the church had decided to go back to church after attending the Christian Faith class. I remembered having breathed a prayer for my husband's class as I drove to piano lessons. Even on busy days God hears our abbreviated prayers.

There is truly much for which we can praise God!

Prayer:
Dear God, inspire a song in my heart. Jesus, by the power of your resurrection raise me up to a new life. Lift me up to praise your name! Amen.

Bread Baking in the Oven

Colossians 4:2-6
Devote yourselves to prayer, being watchful and thankful. And pray for us, too, that God may open a door for our message, so that we may proclaim the mystery of Christ, for which I am in chains. Pray that I may proclaim it clearly, as I should. Be wise in the way you act toward outsiders; make the most of every opportunity. Let your conversation be always full of grace, seasoned with salt, so that you may know how to answer everyone.

For three years my neighbor Betty (not her real name) and I had engaged in only small talk over the backyard fence. Then something happened to change all that! Betty and her husband took in two American Indian foster children, who were in the fifth and seventh grades. To my delight Betty was interested in enrolling her foster children in our Bible school, since they had no previous religious training.

I enlisted the help of congregational members to pray for the success of the Bible school and especially for the conversion of the two foster children and any other unchurched children. I prayed daily that the gospel would come across loud and clear, and that the Holy Spirit would fill their hearts.

Our prayers were answered. Not only was VBS that year a meaningful experience for all who attended, it was especially meaningful to the foster children. The fifth grade girl came home singing all the Jesus songs she had learned. The seventh grader soaked in every Bible story with wide-eyed wonderment. On the final day of the two week session, the seventh grader received a prize for his essay in the upper grades essay contest. His carefully written, three page paper revealed that he knew very clearly what it means to be in God's family.

A couple of weeks later the evangelism team from church went with the VBS teachers to make follow-up visits on the unchurched. I was happy to find Betty at home when our team stopped. While my partners prayed silently, I shared what the children had learned in VBS—the Gospel message—in my own words.

After visiting with her, I asked her if she would like to pray with me, and she agreed. We prayed, thanking God for all the blessings of her family, her husband, and her daughter's upcoming wedding. We prayed for her safe trip to Germany to visit her son. We prayed for the Holy Spirit to guide her husband to love the Lord. When we had finished, there were tears in her eyes. Perhaps no one had ever prayed with her before. After all those years of being close neighbors, we now felt close in the Lord.

I know this visit made an impression on her because, the day we left for Canada, she came out to tell me that she had two loaves of bread baking in the oven for us. I promised to keep praying for her and her family. God had opened the door for the message of the gospel and had shown me how to proclaim his love to my neighbor.

Prayer:

Dear Heavenly Father, give me an open door to bring your message of love to others. Grant me care and concern for others who do not know you. Help me as I proclaim your love. Amen.

Constant Love

Psalm 91:11-16
*For he will command his angels concerning you to guard you in all your ways; they will lift you up in their hands, so that you will not strike your foot against a stone. You will tread upon the lion and the cobra; you will trample the great lion and the serpent. "Because he loves me," says the L*ORD*, "I will rescue him; I will protect him, for he acknowledges my name. He will call upon me, and I will answer him; I will be with him in trouble, I will deliver him and honor him. With long life will I satisfy him and show him my salvation."*

When our family moved from St. Paul, Minnesota to Edmonton, Alberta, Canada, we were given a send-off by my husband's relatives. As I hugged my sister-in-law, Mabel, and said goodbye, she whispered, "We've prayed for your safe journey."

"Thank you," I replied. "Keep on praying."

The day we packed our twenty-four-foot Ryder rental truck, it was a wilting 110 degrees, the hottest day on record in Minnesota for August in fifty years! The drive was a grueling 1,350 miles in three and a half days. I drove the station wagon with three of our children, and Steve, my husband, drove the Ryder truck with the other two children.

Unaccustomed to long distance driving, on the

second day I was exhausted. We had stopped briefly to eat a sandwich in the car and within minutes were back on the road, the bright sunshine beating through the window. With the car on cruise, driving through the flat Saskatchewan countryside became monotonous. Without warning I drifted off to sleep. My thirteen-year-old, sitting in the front seat with me, noticed something was wrong as I meandered into the left lane, heading for the ditch. "Mom! Where are you going?" she blurted out. Startled, I woke up in time to avoid the ditch and a collision with the car in the left lane advancing behind me. Whew! That was a close one!

I praised God for sparing our lives and for allowing my daughter to wake me up in time to avoid an accident. Believe it or not, I fell asleep two other times on the trip up to Canada, and each time I woke up just in time. Upon our safe arrival I wrote to Mabel, thanking her for her continued prayers. But most of all I thanked God for his constant protection. Reread the above passage and, if possible, commit some of it to memory. God promises to be with us in trouble, to deliver us, and to honor us. Praise God for the constant love he shows to those who belong to him!

Prayer:
Dear God, you are not far from each of us. For in you we live and move and have our being. Praise to you, O Lord, God the Father, Son and Holy Spirit. We worship you and praise you in the glory of all your holy angels, now and forever. Amen.

Praying about Little Things

Philippians 4:6,7
Do not be anxious about anything, but in everything, by prayer and petition, with thanksgiving, present your requests to God. And the peace of God, which transcends all understanding, wlll guard your hearts and your minds in Christ Jesus.

It had been a pleasant autumn day in the country. Playing happily in our yard were my five children and two of their schoolmates. Suddenly a large German Shepherd ran into our yard. I screamed at the oldest to get the children into the house. Then I realized that the strange dog was being gentle to the kids, and I recognized it as the neighbor's dog. In spite of its awesome appearance, the dog was as gentle as a cat.

Soon the three older boys and my youngest, five-year-old P. J., were trudging across the three-quarter mile field of oats stubble to return the dog to the next door neighbor. I was worried that P. J. might easily trip and get poked in the face by the sharp stubble.

I was making supper, wondering whether I should

pray about this or whether it was one of those little things that would probably turn out all right anyway. But the Holy Spirit helped me breathe a short prayer, "Jesus, help the boys get back safe." I felt at peace, laying my worries in God's hands.

About twenty minutes later a car drove up. Our neighbor was so grateful to the boys for bringing the dog back that she gave them juice and cookies and a ride home. P. J. was unscathed, even though he had tripped many times and two times fell flat on his face.

Would the boys have gotten back all right even if I hadn't prayed? Possibly, but in either case God deserves the praise and glory. He is in control, protecting and guiding. With God nothing is accidental. Every blessing we receive is a gift of his grace. Prayer keeps us mindful that our blessings come from God. God wants us "in everything," I repeat, "in everything" to present our requests to him (Philippians 4:6). Yes, God answers prayers, for big things and for little things; but even before the answer comes, "the peace of God, which transcends all understanding" floods our hearts.

Prayer:
Dear Jesus, you have borne our griefs and carried our sorrows. You have borne the sin of us all and the punishment for our sins. You have in mind for us total joy and the marvelous peace that passes understanding. Help us habitually to take all requests, big and small, to your throne of grace, that our lives may be full of praise to you continually. Amen.

My Purpose in Life

Titus 2:11-14
For the grace of God that brings salvation has appeared to all men. It teaches us to say "No" to ungodliness and worldly passions, and to live self-controlled, upright and godly lives in this present age, while we wait for the blessed hope—the glorious appearing of our great God and Savior, Jesus Christ, who gave himself for us to redeem us from all wickedness and to purify for himself a people that are his very own, eager to do what is good.

When we moved to Canada, I was on a "no-work" visa. Even though my kids were now all in school, I could not work. I proceeded to write a book, but I often wondered what other purpose God had in mind for me. It became clear to me one night as I accompanied the church's evangelism team on a call to a family with four young children. The living room was very cluttered, so I suggested we meet in the kitchen where we could sit around the table. As we talked, we found that the parents had really not attended church much since their marriage.

I wasn't sure what I was going to say, but I knew that my two team members were praying for me. I began drawing a picture of a man carrying a burden. As I began explaining the burden as worries, cares and sins, soon all of the four children were gathering around the table to watch me, including the six-month-old baby on her mother's lap. I explained that we could go through life trying to carry the burden of life's problems on our own, or we could have Jesus carry our burdens. I drew a picture of the cross with the man's burden tied to it. "Jesus bore our sins for us," I said.

Everyone sat very quietly to listen. Then my team

partner, a lively older woman, told a poignant story to explain the good news of the gospel:

> A king once owned a beautiful island where everything was perfect. One day the king announced that the island was to be kept perfect, and the first one who did anything wrong would be executed. Time passed and one man did something wrong. He was taken to prison to await his execution.
>
> On the day of the scheduled execution, the guard came to get him. The man was very sad and told the guard that he knew what was going to happen to him that day. The man was taken to the king. The king announced that he would not have to be executed.
>
> "Why?" the man asked. "Did you change the rules?"
>
> "No," answered the king. "My son was executed in your place, and you better be grateful!"

The family listened intently. I asked if they would mind if we said a prayer. We prayed for their two children who were ill. We prayed, thanking God for sending Jesus to take *our* place and die for *our* sins. We prayed that God would tenderly care for their family.

As we left their home, I felt I had the answer to what my purpose was. Whether I was in Canada, Australia, Africa or the United States, the answer would be the same—to tell others about Jesus.

Prayer:
Jesus, give me oil in my lamp. Keep me burning with the message that you are the light of the world. Please light the way for my witnessing. Thank you, Jesus. Amen.

Make My Life an Alleluia!

Leave It in the Lord's Hands

John 20:26-28
Though the doors were locked, Jesus came and stood among them and said, "Peace be with you!" Then he said to Thomas, "Put your finger here; see my hands. Reach out your hand and put it into my side. Stop doubting and believe."
Thomas said to him, "My Lord and my God!"

A friend of mine used to write all her worries down on slips of paper and tie them up in a cloth bag. Then she would pray about her worries and wouldn't think of them anymore. When she opened the bag months later, usually all her worries had been solved. Letting go of our worries like that frees us. We admit that we can't handle them, and we trust that God is able and willing to take care of them for us.

Leave it in the Lord's hands. God's hands are big, capable and powerful. In the first chapter of John we read how God's Son created the universe. God's strong hands formed the world and spun the planets into space, and God's gentle hands designed each one of us in the womb before we were born. God's hands are powerful enough to help us and gentle enough to care for us.

In Matthew 11:28 Jesus beckons to us: "Come to me, all you who are weary and burdened, and I will give you rest." Jesus' hands are reaching out to us.

And Jesus' hands are loving hands, wounded hands—hands once nailed to a cross to show the full extent of his love. In his wounds we can hide and find peace and pardon for our souls. What can you do about the thing bothering you right now? Leave it in the Lord's hands!

The Lord's hands are big, capable and strong. They are gentle and loving, and they reach out to us, ready to help. In our Lord's wounded hands we can find forgiveness and peace for our souls.

Prayer:
Jesus, my Lord and my God, grant that I will find healing in your wounded hands and side. Help me to leave my worries in your powerful and loving hands. I praise you, Jesus, for taking care of me. Amen.

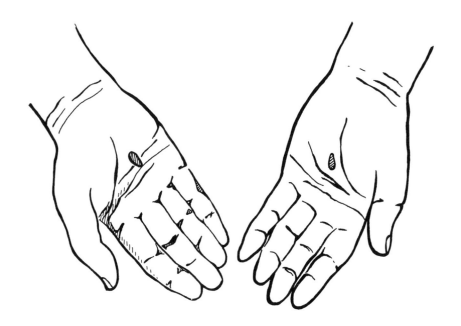

Leave it in the Lord's hands

The Way Home

Hebrews 3:1
Therefore, holy brothers, who share in the heavenly calling, fix your thoughts on Jesus. . . .

Recently I received a letter from our former Nebraska parishioners. It described a tragic tractor accident that killed a middle-aged woman, one of our former members. Only a year before, I had visited with her when she came to Minneapolis for her husband's back surgery. I began to cry as I read the newspaper clipping of her accident and funeral service. She was such a friendly and optimistic woman.

Later that same day my twelve-year-old and ten-year-old children sang a song that cheered my spirit:

The blind man sat by the road and he cried,
The blind man sat by the road and he cried,
Show me the way! Show me the way! Show me the way!
The way to go home.

Jesus sat by the road and he cried,
Jesus sat by the road and he cried,

"I am the Way! I am the Way! I am the Way!
The Way to go home!"

It occurred to me that the lady who was run over by a tractor knew the way to go home. She was a joyful Christian who had her thoughts fixed on Jesus. Through his grace she experienced the opening of heaven's portals at her death and the beginning of a beautiful life that never ends.

It is sometimes hard to fix our thoughts on Jesus. There are so many other things to think about—the buying of groceries, clothes, and other things; doctor and dentist appointments; our children's sports and recreational activities. But we know that we as holy brothers and sisters in Christ share in a heavenly calling. With our thoughts fixed on Jesus and his cross and open tomb, we will readily share our joy with others and finally find our eternal rest.

Prayer:
Hold thou thy cross before my closing eyes,
Shine through the gloom and point me to the skies.
Heaven's morning breaks, and earth's vain shadows flee;
In life, in death, O Lord, abide with me. Amen.

A Quiet Place

Mark 6:30-31
The apostles gathered around Jesus and reported to him all they had done and taught. Then, because so many people were coming and going that they did not even have a chance to eat, he said to them, "Come with me by yourselves to a quiet place and get some rest."

As a college student, I had the fantastic opportunity to take a study tour in Europe. Six thousand feet up in the Swiss Alps, I strolled by myself, delighted to pick flowers in the Alpine meadow. There was a sweet silence, broken only by the gentle tinkling of cowbells in the distant pastures. The air had a fresh, pure scent. The tunes of "How Sweet the Name of Jesus Sounds" and "Tis Good Lord to Be Here" floated into my consciousness. The delicate branches of the spring green pines dangled in the slight breeze. It was a breathtaking experience, a moment of quiet and rest.

Amidst the hustle and bustle of daily life, Jesus calls us to come with him to a quiet place where we can get some rest. Remember the story of the stilling of the storm. Even in the midst of the storms of this life, we can rest knowing that Jesus "is in our boat." Jesus gives us rest. He is our hide-away.

In Exodus 33:14 the Lord promised Moses, "My Presence will go with you, and I will give you rest."

In Matthew 11:28,29 Jesus promises, "Come to me, all you who are weary and burdened, and I will give you rest. Take my yoke upon you and learn from me, for I am gentle and humble in heart, and you will find rest for your souls."

In Hebrews 4:9,10 we read: "There remains, then, a Sabbath-rest for the people of God; for anyone who enters God's rest also rests from his own work, just as God did from his."

In Revelation 14:13 we see heaven pictured as the final rest. "Then I heard a voice from heaven say, 'Write: Blessed are the dead who die in the Lord from now on.' 'Yes,' says the Spirit, 'they will rest from their labor, for their deeds will follow them.'"

How can we find this quiet place with Jesus? One way is through private devotions and prayer. Another is through Christian women's retreats. Another is through going to church. The singing, the reading of the Word, and the personal assurance of forgiveness of sins in the Lord's Supper give us a quiet place—a rest from our labors.

Prayer:

O day of rest and gladness,
O day of joy and light,
O balm of care and sadness,
Most beautiful, most bright,
On thee the high and lowly
Before the eternal throne
Sing, "Holy, Holy, Holy,"
To the great Three in One.

New graces ever gaining,
From this our day of rest,
We reach the rest remaining,
To spirits of the blest.
To Holy Ghost be praises,
To Father, and to Son;
The church her voice upraises
To Thee, blest Three in One.
                     Amen.

Cocoa on My Bible

I Corinthians 1:4-9
I always thank God for you because of his grace given you in Christ Jesus. For in him you have been enriched in every way—in all your speaking and in all your knowledge—because our testimony about Christ was confirmed in you. Therefore you do not lack any spiritual gift as you eagerly wait for our Lord Jesus Christ to be revealed. He will keep you strong to the end, so that you will be blameless on the day of our Lord Jesus Christ. God, who has called you into fellowship with his Son Jesus Christ our Lord, is faithful.

At first I was angry when I found that one of the kids, while doing memory work, had spilled cocoa on a page of my Bible, making it difficult to read the words. Then I began to think perhaps there was a lesson I could learn from this. First, I was glad that my children were reading the Bible, and that it was not just a show piece on the coffee table. Second, I realized that perhaps I was getting too attached to that copy of the Bible. I was very proud of it because it had a wide selection of maps and pictures. It was a pictorial Bible with an index and lists in the back, and it cost a lot of money. I remembered some words of Martin Luther describing the Bible as "the cradle in which Christ is laid." Perhaps I was too attached to my expensive book and the fact that I knew many Bible passages by heart *with* the exact reference. Maybe I was making too much of "the cradle."

Many Christians gradually fall away, thinking that memorizing the Bible and talking about God is the same as talking to God and having a personal relationship with him. All of these outward things are important, but the real essence of our faith is that, through his word, *God* by his grace and faithfulness *holds us.*

The real evidence of faith is revealed when the totally dependent and helpless soul cries out softly, "Jesus!" At difficult times, in the frightening dark of a stormy night, when faced with an impending car crash, when lying on a bed, sick and in pain, the soul cries out, "Jesus! Help me!" and God takes over. He assures us that he was always there, that he is very near and that he will hold us. Our very faith in him is a gift, given by him. When we are weak, then he is strong!

Prayer:
Dear God, always protect me from the sin of pride. Keep me from merely treasuring the Bible as a book. Rather lead me through the Bible to treasure Jesus, who is one with you and the Spirit. Thank you for the gift of faith through your Holy Spirit. Hold me in my proud times, in my doubting times, in my angry times, in my repentant times, but most of all, hold me tightest right before my death. I pray this in Jesus' name, because of his innocent suffering and death for me and his holy precious blood shed for me. Amen.

Running the Race with Patience

Hebrews 12:1-3
Therefore, since we are surrounded by such a great cloud of witnesses, let us throw off everything that hinders and the sin that so easily entangles, and let us run with perseverance the race marked out for us. Let us fix our eyes on Jesus, the author and perfecter of our faith, who for the joy set before him endured the cross, scorning its shame, and sat down at the right hand of the throne of God. Consider him who endured such opposition from sinful men, so that you will not grow weary and lose heart.

Sometimes I become discouraged with the menial tasks that go along with being a homemaker and mother; you know, the little monotonous things like tying your child's shoe, cleaning the oven, taking out the trash, scrubbing out the tub. One day I attended a Lutheran women's rally. The speaker talked about doing everything to the glory of God. Then I discovered that it's not just the doing of these things that is important, but *how* one does them. Singing hymns of praise to Jesus as one goes about these daily tasks takes the humdrum out of doing them and is also more pleasing to God, who loves the *cheerful* giver.

In addition Jesus reminds us in the judgment day passages of Matthew 25, "I tell you the truth, whatever you did for one of the least of these brothers of mine, you did for me" (v. 40).

At night, when I am worn out from a busy day and finally get my little boys tucked in bed and prayers said, one of them invariably asks for a drink of water. At first I grudgingly head for the kitchen. Then I remember Jesus' words in Matthew 10:42: "And if anyone gives even a cup of cold water to one of these little ones because he is my disciple, I tell you the truth, he will certainly not lose his reward." My steps lighten and a smile covers my face as I give the drink of water to my little one, just as if I were giving it to the Lord!

When times are difficult, I am reminded of Galatians 6:9: "Let us not become weary in doing good, for at the proper time we will reap a harvest if we do not give up."

Sometimes the harvest may be immediate. The other day my five year old asked me to play the "Snoopy Card Game" with him. I looked up from my typewriter and thought of all the work I had to do and how that game would blow an hour of my precious time. Then I thought of how important this time with MOM would be to him, so I consented. The rewards were immediate—seeing my five year old smile from ear to ear.

Prayer:
Dear God, don't let me become weary in doing good. Help me do everything to your glory as if I were doing it for you. Put a song in my heart as I go about my daily tasks. Jesus, you endured the agony and the shame of the cross for me. Help me endure any difficulties with the strength that you provide. Hold the glory of life everlasting before my eyes as I run the race of life. Amen.

Loving My Teenager

Matthew 18:21,22
Then Peter came to Jesus and asked, "Lord, how many times shall I forgive my brother when he sins against me? Up to seven times?" Jesus answered, "I tell you, not seven times, but seventy-seven times."

Teen years are trying for teens and their parents. I was particularly upset with one of my teenagers one day. The next day I noticed a name button from vacation Bible school several years before. It had my teenager's name in small letters at the top with "GOD LOVES YOU!" in bold letters across the center. Even if I was temporarily upset, I still loved my child. More important, God's love, since baptism at age two weeks, had been constant.

Arguments would come and go. There were days of relative peace, but then fighting would break out again. Frequently heard lines were: "You're treating me like a baby." "I can take care of myself." "You don't understand me." The sentences cut deep and, if one were to take them personally, they really hurt!

We tried to keep the conversations calm and the voices low to discuss things rationally. We had to keep in mind that the rebellious stage that teens go through is normal and to take the accusations, like "You don't love me," with a grain of salt. Most of the time, by some miracle, apologies would come, but sometimes they wouldn't. At those times I would say something like this: "I am a person and I had my feelings hurt. God loves me just as he loves you. No matter what you say or do, I will always love you." The apologies would come the next day.

It is very hard to forgive someone when they do not say, "I'm sorry." At those difficult times I look to God for a model of love. He forgives me all the time, even if I don't say, "I'm sorry." He loves me even when I am unlovable. I am certain there were times as a teenager I should have said, "I'm sorry," to my parents. I didn't realize until I was a parent myself how I must have hurt their feelings, but God's abounding love covered it all like a blanket. Through God's steadfast love and grace, I can forgive my children again and again.

Prayer:

Dear God, fill me again with your abundant love. Give me the fruits of the Holy Spirit—love, joy, peace, patience, kindness, goodness, faithfulness, gentleness, self-control. Forgive my sins and help me to forgive my children the way you forgive me. Amen.

Make My Life an Alleluia!

Always under the Umbrella

II Corinthians 5:14,15
For Christ's love compels us, because we are convinced that one died for all, and therefore all died. And he died for all, that those who live should no longer live for themselves but for him who died for them and was raised again.

It was one of those days when nothing goes as planned. We had invited the choir to rehearse at our house, with refreshments to follow the rehearsal. I cleaned the house all day. It looked pretty good, but an hour before the twenty-five people were to arrive, my three boys ran in and out of the kitchen with muddy boots from playing outside. Then the dog got stomach sick, not once, but three times. While I was busy mopping the floor again, a car drove up and notified us that our neighbor's cattle were running down the road at top speed. While my husband and boys ran over to tell the neighbors about their cattle, the dog got sick again. There weren't enough chairs set up for the choir, and then the doorbell rang! Someone had arrived early. I looked at the sink full of dishes. I had hoped to have those finished. Things weren't going as I had planned. I took a couple of deep breaths and answered the door. Soon the rest of the guests arrived all at once.

As we sat down for opening devotions I was a bundle of nerves, and I felt guilty for yelling at my kids and blowing my cool before the guests arrived. As I was trying to regain my composure so I could sing, a Bible verse I had tucked away in my heart when I was taking confirmation instructions came to my mind. It was a short verse, but it was all that I needed to feel right with God again: "And he [Jesus] died for all" (2 Corinthians 5:15). "Jesus died for me," I thought to myself. That is all I need to know to put my mind at peace and to assure me that I am dearly loved by God.

Things in life do not always go as planned. Even our own death may come suddenly, not as we had planned. We may not have enough time to say a prayer or say goodbye to our loved ones. But God has assured us that we are always under the umbrella of his grace because Jesus died for us and rose again. Paul says in Romans 14:8, "If we live, we live to the Lord; and if we die, we die to the Lord. So, whether we live or die, we belong to the Lord." Because we belong to God, we live under the umbrella of his grace, always living in the forgiveness of sins, even if we would be sinning at the moment of death. Knowing that God sustains us with his grace can also help to calm us down when everything seems to go wrong and we lose our cool. We can say confidently, "I am a child of God. I live in the forgiveness of sins, always under the umbrella of God's grace."

Prayer:

God, please forgive all my sins because Jesus died for me. Help me to stay in your grace now and forever. Assure me that I am your child always. Amen.

Christ died for all.
2 *Corinthians 5:15*

Yes, No, Wait

John 14:13,14
And I will do whatever you ask in my name, so that the Son may bring glory to the Father. You may ask me for anything in my name, and I will do it.

In the account of the raising of Lazarus in John 11, Mary and Martha, the sisters of Lazarus, sent word to Jesus that Lazarus was sick. Jesus knew that Lazarus was sick but he waited two days before coming to see him. When he finally came, Lazarus was already dead. Mary was disappointed. She had put her faith in Jesus' power to heal her brother. Now he was dead. What a disappointment! She said, "Lord, if you had been here, my brother would not have died." But Jesus in his wisdom waited until Lazarus was dead in order to show His power over death so that he and his Father would be glorified.

A young man at our church experienced great pain for two years because of an accident at work involving the muscles of his neck, arms and shoulder. He prayed often for a cure or relief. He went to many doctors and finally ended up taking a course on how to deal with pain. His wife and his young five-year-old son prayed often for him. He was unable to go back to work at his construction job, so his wife worked long hours to support the family.

One night four of us from our prayer group at church went to his house to pray for him. We prayed that God's will would be done, that if it was God's will to heal him, that would be done; but if it was not God's will, that our friend would have the strength and the patience to bear the pain. We left his house that night believing that God could indeed heal him, if that were his will. The following week we found that the pain level was about the same. Like Mary, we were disappointed. But the young man shared his faith with us. God had made it clear to him that there was a reason for his pain and that he could use it to glorify God. The pain was a constant reminder to the young man of the tortures and pain in hell waiting for those who do not believe in Jesus. It also reminded him of the day when there would be sweet relief from all pain and suffering in heaven. The pain made the young man a bold witness for Jesus, his Savior. He witnessed to others in the pain management group concerning the grace Jesus had given him in his life. He was eager to share his faith with his neighbors, and they were amazed at his deep trust in God despite adversity.

Some day Jesus may take the pain away. But if not, the real answer to those many prayers for healing will take place in heaven. There Jesus promised us a perfect body "like unto his glorious body." Does God hear every prayer? He certainly does! But he may have a different way of answering our prayer than what we expect. Moreover, we know that God has our best welfare in mind, and that his answer will glorify his name!

Prayer:
Dear Heavenly Father, glorify your name and the name of your Son, Jesus, in every answer to my prayers. May your most holy will be done in my life. Amen.

Lists, Lists, Lists

Hebrews 7:25
Therefore he [Jesus] is able to save completely those who come to God through him, because he always lives to intercede for them.

Lists, lists, lists! I get tired of them, but I keep writing lists of things to do. After a while they become almost a burden because I feel compelled to cross things off when they are done, and, if I have nothing to cross off, I feel like I'm not accomplishing anything.

I'm thankful our faith is one area where we never have to make lists. Jesus did it all, everything necessary for our salvation. We do not have to do a number of good deeds to get to heaven. It is all a free gift because of Jesus. In fact, even our faith in Jesus is a gift through the power of the Holy Spirit. This is one area of our life in which we may lie back and relax, knowing that Jesus has saved us completely.

If we lack peace of mind, it may be that we are worried about death. If we die, will we make it to heaven? This is a fearful worry, terrifying because the alternative, everlasting punishment, an eternity without God or anything good, is most frightening. But God's Word helps us to see that we don't have to fear death. Jesus has already won eternal life for us. Jesus tells us that whoever believes in him has eternal life already.

Former first lady, Nancy Reagan, told an evangelism congress about her father's death. He had not been a regular church-goer, and, when he was about to die, the eternity of separation from God stretched like a wide chasm before him. At night he would not lie down to sleep, but moved from chair to chair to keep awake in case he would die. He had no peace. Nancy prayed for him and tried to witness to him of her source of peace in Jesus Christ. Finally the day before he died, a chaplain visited him and shared the gospel. Nancy believes he died peacefully, resting in the Lord.

What has Jesus done to save us? First, he led a perfect life in our place, fulfilling the demands of the law for us. Then, "HE DIED FOR ALL" (2 Corinthians

5:15). Jesus bore our sin on the cross: "And the Lord has laid on him [Jesus] the iniquity of us all" (Isaiah 53:6). Our iniquity is that evil nature of ours, our sinful flesh that rebels against God, with the resulting sins and guilt.

Also, Jesus took the punishment for our sins. "The punishment that brought us peace was upon him [Jesus]" (Isaiah 53:5). The punishment was for our sins. Isaiah 53:5 tells us, "But he [Jesus] was pierced for our transgressions, he was crushed for our iniquities; the punishment that brought us peace was upon him, and by his wounds we are healed."

Jesus also took our guilt: "The Lord makes his [Jesus'] life a guilt offering" (Isaiah 53:10). Jesus experienced separation from God (hell) in our place when he was on the cross, crying out, "My God, my God, why have you forsaken me?" (Matthew 27:46). Jesus shed HIS precious blood for the forgiveness of everyone's sins, as we read in Matthew 26:28, "This is my blood of the covenant, which is poured out for many for the forgiveness of sins." In 1 Peter 1:18,19 we read, "For you know that it was not with perishable things such as silver or gold that you were redeemed. . .but with the precious blood of Christ, a lamb without blemish or defect."

God does things perfectly. He does things completely. Only God could think of the perfect sacrifice, the sacrifice of his only Son. Jesus did it all. Jesus completed our salvation. When God looks at us, he sees us as holy, covered with Jesus' righteousness, the white robe of holiness that we receive through his bleeding and dying for us. Colossians 1:22 reads, "But now he [God] has reconciled you by Christ's physical body through death to present you *holy* in his sight, without blemish and free from accusation. . . ."

Prayer:
God, thank you for the peace of mind that comes from knowing that Jesus did it all for me. He died for me so I can live forever. God, please help me to lie back in your loving arms and trust in you for eternal life. Amen.

More than Enough

John 6:10-13
Jesus said, "Have the people sit down." There was plenty of grass in that place, and the men sat down, about five thousand of them. Jesus then took the loaves, gave thanks, and distributed to those who were seated as much as they wanted. He did the same with the fish. When they had all had enough to eat, he said to his disciples, "Gather the pieces that are left over. Let nothing be wasted." So they gathered them and filled twelve baskets with the pieces of the five barley loaves left over by those who had eaten.

Do you worry that you will not have enough money to make it through the month? Do you worry that you will not have enough money for your children to go to college? Do you worry that your teenager will not have enough strength to withstand peer pressure? Do you worry that you will not be a good enough mother for your children? Do you worry that you will not have enough faith to die?

In Philippians 4:19 Paul says, "And my God will meet all your needs according to his glorious riches in Christ Jesus." In the account of the feeding of the 5,000, Jesus did the miraculous. He fed more than 5,000 people with five small loaves and two small fish, and there were twelve baskets of bread left over. Jesus had supplied them with "as much as they wanted." But there was still more than enough.

Friends of mine, Paul and Andrea, had just returned from the mission field in New Guinea. They were caring for their four children, the youngest one being very ill. Paul was attending graduate school while Andrea took care of the children. There was little food to eat, and Andrea was prepared to serve soup on Thanksgiving Day. But as that day drew near, one of their neighbors, out of generosity, gave them a turkey for their Thanksgiving dinner. At the same time Andrea's name was drawn as the winner of a free turkey in two local grocery drawings. There was more than enough turkey. In fact, they ended up having a lot of company over for Thanksgiving to share their abundance. Andrea and her family had more than enough through Jesus' bountiful provision.

Will you and your children have more than enough? No matter how few material things we have, we have our priceless Treasure, Jesus, and the treasures of his Word.

Do you have enough faith to die and get to heaven? Even Christians worry about this at times. Whenever feelings of inadequacy come over us, we need only to look upward to Jesus, who led a perfect, righteous life for us. His death, his precious shed blood and his glorious resurrection are the PERFECT means for us to be saved. Jesus has done enough. We do not need to work to earn salvation. We are saved by his grace. In HIS GRACE and the strength of HIS POWER in our lives, there is MORE THAN ENOUGH to meet our needs.

Prayer:
Jesus, you are my wealth and riches. You are my treasure and joy. Assure me through your presence in my daily walk and through your Word and Holy Communion, that with you, Jesus, I have more than enough. Thank you, Jesus! Amen.

Praise God at All Times

Romans 8:28
And we know that in all things God works for the good of those who love him, who have been called according to his purpose.

(The following is a puppet show for two characters, Mr. Happy and Mr. Sad.)

Narrator: What makes you happy? What makes you sad?
Mr. H: Hi! I'm Mr. Happy!
Mr. S: And I'm Mr. Sad.
Mr. H: I'm very happy today because today's my birthday and I got lots of presents and we had cake and soda and....
Mr. S: And I'm very sad today. I'm so sad that hearing you tell about how happy you are makes me feel even sadder.
Mr. H: What are you sad about?
Mr. S: Well, because of a lot of things. First, I got out of bed and stubbed my toe, and for lunch I ate a pickle and peanut butter sand-

Make My Life an Alleluia!

	wich, and I got sick to my stomach, and then the chain came off my bike, and my Dad couldn't fix it and then....
Mr. H:	Hold on for a moment. I brought along a sign that might help.
	(Holds up a sign that says "Praise God!") Maybe we can thank and praise God for your day.
Mr. S:	My sad day?
Mr. H:	That's right. Your sad day.
Mr. S:	But why would God give me a sad day?
Mr. H:	Well, we know God loves us at all times, and that God works everything out for our good, so there must be a reason for your sad day.... (pause)
Mr. S:	I just thought of a reason.
Mr. H:	You have?
Mr. S:	Well, when I got sick to my stomach it was awful; but Johnny, my friend, came over with some comic books to cheer me up. You know, if Johnny ever gets sick I'm going to do something nice for him, because I know how it feels now to have the stomach flu.
Mr. H:	That's right. You can sympathize with others. Praise God! (waves sign)
Mr. S:	And you know the chain on my bike that Dad couldn't fix? Well, we asked Mr. Smith next door if he could, and do you know what? I heard Dad and Mr. Smith talking about how Mr. Smith could do a good job fixing bikes. Then Mr. Smith said he wished he could do something to fix up his life, because he had

	made so many mistakes, and I heard my Dad tell him that Jesus could fix anything and make his life brand new again.
Mr. H:	That's great! You see, God does have reasons for our sad days.
Mr. S:	Could I borrow your sign?
Mr. H:	Sure. In fact I have two. So you can keep that one.
Mr. S:	Thank you! You know what? I already feel happier praising God.

I am certain that you, my readers, can easily substitute your own examples of sad times for those listed in this little play. Next time the car breaks down, the dishes pile up, the boss criticizes you, your child is sick, think of how in *all* things God works for the good of those who love him. Think of how this can be used to his glory. Even our worst sadness, death, is but the door to eternal life. Praise God at all times!

Prayer:

"Praise be to the God and Father of our Lord Jesus Christ, the Father of compassion and the God of all comfort, who comforts us in all our troubles, so that we can comfort those in any trouble with the comfort we ourselves have received from God" (2 Corinthians 1:3,4). Thank you, God, for happy times and sad times. Help me to praise you for how you work out *all* things for my good. Amen.

Not Just a Spectator

I Corinthians 11:26
For whenever you eat this bread and drink this cup, you proclaim the Lord's death until he comes.

It was a long drive to the little country church where my husband was preaching that day. I settled back into the rear pew and felt very much like a spectator. The organist warmed up, hitting all the wrong notes and muttering something about not knowing how to play the music. Someone came up to her to encourage her. The members were talking audibly to each other before the service began. Since I did not know anyone, I sat back and watched.

About half way through the service, I realized that it was a Communion Sunday. I felt very unprepared. I had been sitting through the service like a spectator, and all at once I realized I could be a participant. Jesus was inviting me to come to his Supper! I knew I should attend, but my faith had been in a slump period, and I didn't feel ready to go up there.

While I was wrestling with the idea of going forward or sitting back unnoticed, the usher came to the pew in front of me and asked if I intended to go to Communion. I prayed a quick prayer, "God, prepare my heart as I walk down the aisle."

God, who is faithful to his own, supplied me with faith and Scripture as I walked the long aisle to the front of the church. "And he took bread, gave thanks and broke it, and gave it to them, saying, 'This is my body given for you; do this in remembrance of me'" (Luke 22:19). "Then he took the cup, gave thanks and offered it to them, saying, 'Drink from it, all of you. This is my blood of the covenant, which is poured out for many for the forgiveness of sins'" (Matthew 26:27,28). "'Do this, whenever you drink it, in remembrance of me'" (1 Corinthians 11:25).

I came back rejoicing in God's love. You see, God is faithful, and when we are weak, he is strong. I came back to the pew, full of peace and much closer to Jesus. The whole day was beautiful, and I felt much more love for my husband, children and those I met at the coffee hour after church. In fact, I can truthfully say that the times I attend the Lord's Supper at church, I feel much more refreshed and more joyful. There is an indescribable deep peace and feeling of being forgiven and accepted by God that comes from Holy Communion.

We should attend the Lord's Supper every time it is offered in order to receive the blessings it gives. Christ brings the past, his suffering, shedding of blood and death, right up to the present. It makes our faith alive and current. He revives us with the forgiveness of sins through his death and resurrection for us. A Christian writer once said, "We should attend the Lord's Supper as if we were going to die, so that when we die, it will be as if we were going to the Lord's Supper."

Prayer:

Dear Jesus, forgive me for neglecting your Word or Sacraments. Renew my heart through the power of the Holy Spirit so that I may long to come to you and lay down my burdens and be refreshed. I long for that eternal communion in heaven with you, Jesus. Thank you for your Holy Supper to strengthen me on my pilgrimage here on earth. Amen.

Like a Little Child

Luke 18:15-17
People were also bringing babies to Jesus to have him touch them. When the disciples saw this, they rebuked them. But Jesus called the children to him and said, "Let the little children come to me, and do not hinder them, for the kingdom of God belongs to such as these. I tell you the truth, anyone who will not receive the kingdom of God like a little child will never enter it."

I love baby showers. When I was expecting my children, I was given beautiful showers by our parishes in Nebraska and by the ladies' group at our church in St. Paul, Minnesota. I especially enjoy giving baby showers. Recently, while preparing for the entertainment for one of my showers for a teacher's wife at our Lutheran school, I came across some lovely lullabye songs for babies. As I sang these songs, a quiet kind of childlike peace came over me. I remembered singing to my children when they were babies and watching their lovely long eyelashes gradually close over their eyes in peaceful slumbers. One of my favorites was to the tune of "Rock-a-bye Baby."

Jesus Loves Children[1]
Jesus loves children,
Jesus loves me,
Jesus loves you with love tenderly,
Jesus loves all, no matter how small,
That's why I love Jesus better than all.

Another more recent lullabye I like is from "Psalty's Sleepytime Helpers":[2]

It's time for sleepy time.
It's time to rest your head,

To snuggle up and get cozy in your bed,
To dream of happy things
Of how much God loves you
Cause you're His special child
It's sleepytime.

Perhaps you can remember back to when someone sang to you as a child, but even if you can't, perhaps you can remember back to a feeling of being loved totally and completely and being cared for by loving parents and a loving God. But even if that is not possible, it is not too late to become a child again and to experience what it is like to have serene peace in the Heavenly Father's care. Jesus said that anyone who would not receive the kingdom of God like a little child would never enter it. You can receive Jesus and eternal life like a little child through the Holy Spirit. The Holy Spirit, through the word of God, assures you that the good news truly is real and, yes, you can lean back, close your eyes, and let your loving God rock you to sleep. You can feel that special peace and freedom from worries and cares that a little baby feels. You are in God's hands. God loves you. You are his special child. Relax in his loving arms now and forever!

Prayer:

What a Friend we have in Jesus,
All our sins and griefs to bear!
What a privilege to carry
Everything to God in prayer!
Oh, what peace we often forfeit,
Oh, what needless pain we bear,
All because we do not carry
Everything to God in prayer!

Are we weak and heavy laden,
Cumbered with a load of care?
Precious Savior, still our refuge
Take it to the Lord in prayer.
Do thy friends despise, forsake thee?
Take it to the Lord in prayer;
In his arms He'll take and shield thee,
Thou wilt find a solace there.

1. From A Child's Garden of Song, Copyright 1949 Concordia Publishing House. Reprinted by permission from CPH.
2. "It's Time for Sleepytime" by Ernie Rettino and Debbie Rettino copyright 1986 Rettino/Kerner Pub. (Adm. by Maranatha! Music.) All rights reserved. International copyright secured. Used by permis-

Free! Free Indeed!

John 8:31,32,36
Jesus said, "If you hold to my teaching, you are really my disciples. Then you will know the truth, and the truth will set you free. . . . So if the Son sets you free, you will be free indeed."

What does it mean to be free? What does it mean to be free to be a good wife or mother? The trap that most Christian mothers fall into is worry. They may be excessively worried about the health or safety of their children or teenagers. They may worry about their past sins and whether they are right before God. They may be slaves to the sin of over-anxiousness about their children or slaves to the guilt and fear of punishment that comes with sin. There may be "shudder" sins—sins too terrible even to talk about—that lurk in the past or that plague the thoughts of the outwardly good mother. What happens when these worries become immense? The wife and mother is not free to give love to herself, her husband or her children.

But if the Son sets us free, we will be free indeed. First Jesus promises to set us free from sin. He assures us further that he will be with us always and take care of us. We can cast our cares on him because he cares for us. We can give him our children's problems, too. In the hymn, "A Mighty Fortress Is Our God," I often wondered what the "little word" was that can fell the devil and his might. (See hymn below.) That word is the Word, "Jesus." Jesus makes us free. He is all we need. That Word whispered on our dying lips is all we need to usher us into eternal life. Jesus has made us holy. Hebrews 10:10 reads, "We have been made holy through the sacrifice of the body of Jesus Christ once for all."

The sins and guilt of the past or present need not enslave us. We have the name of Jesus, the righteousness of Jesus, the perfect sacrifice of Jesus on Calvary's cross. We can relax in the freedom of what Jesus has done for us. We do not have to do a certain number of good works to get to heaven. Our acceptance before God does not depend on us, whether we say certain prayers or have good thoughts. Our holiness depends on Jesus. When we know Jesus and trust in him, we are free from the curse of sin, free to live for Jesus, free to smile and trust in him, free to be utterly happy, free to be loving wives and mothers who are full of loving surprises for our families. We are free from the fear of death so that we can really live and be radiant for the Lord and our families.

Prayer:
Dear Jesus, thank you for setting me free. Help me to radiate your freedom so that I can share your love with my family. Amen.

> Though devils all the world should fill, all eager to devour us,
> We tremble not; we fear no ill; they shall not overpower us.
> This world's prince may still scowl fierce as he will.
> He can harm us none; he's judged; the deed is done.
> One little word can fell him.

Fear Knots and Fear Nots

Luke 2:10-11
But the angel said to them, "Do not be afraid. I bring you good news of great joy that will be for all the people. Today in the town of David a Savior has been born to you; he is Christ the Lord."

Imagine a clothesline with knots tied in it. Now close your eyes and think back in your personal memory computer to the fear knots of your childhood, adolescence and adulthood. What were your fears and worries?

What were your worries as a child: fear of leaving home to attend school, fear of being laughed at, fear of not being chosen to play softball, fear of the dark, fear of falling off your bike?

What were your fears as an adolescent: fear of not being accepted by your peers, fear of being the only one without a date, fear of not looking attractive enough, fear of becoming an old maid, fear of not making it through college or vocational school, fear of not finding a job?

What are your fears as an adult: fear of not finding a mate; fear of divorce; fear of being lonely; fear of losing a child through an accident or illness; fear of inadequacy on the job; fear of cancer; fear of muscular dystrophy; fear of A.I.D.S.; fear of raising children in a world of evil, sexual impurity, and growing T.V. and movie menace; fear of growing old; fear of judgment day; fear of death itself?

To you in all of these fears comes the message of the angel on that first Christmas night: "Fear not!" (KJV) "I bring you good news of great joy that will be for all the people. Today in the town of David a Savior has been born to you; he is Christ the Lord." Fear not! What a perfect answer to your fear knots!

The angel brought good news of great joy. You need some good news in this drab world. And great joy! Wow! You need some joy around here! You want to laugh and really enjoy life, but you often are burdened by your own fears. However, you can rejoice again, because the Savior has been born for you! Christ, the promised one, the long awaited Savior, has come! And he will come back again!

He is Christ *the Lord*, God of heaven and earth, Lord of all your fears! He has gone through fears and through death and hell itself for you. He came alive again, victorious over all of them. Jesus is Lord, and he has all power in heaven and on earth.

So fear not! Lay your fears at Jesus' feet and let him take over. Then praise him right now for coming to earth to be your Savior, filling you with good news of great joy. Praise him! And then go out there and tell all the people that they can be joyful, they can laugh again, and they can be freed from their fears because a Savior has been born, CHRIST THE LORD. GREAT JOY!

Prayer:
Jesus, I praise you for flooding my drab life of fears with your joy. Thank you for taking my fears and for giving me your joy and peace to take their place in my heart. Help me to tell the people at my office, at work, at home and everywhere the good news of great joy. Amen.

The Most Satisfying Work

Daniel 12:3
Those who are wise will shine like the brightness of the heavens, and those who lead many to righteousness, like the stars forever and ever.

During World War II a ship sailing in the Pacific was loaded with marines. One man aboard was a Christian and one day approached his officer with a problem. He could not get any of the men to join a Bible study. The officer told him to pray for someone on board to do the work of gathering people with him. The man soon had a partner, a new Christian, who together with the sailor worked at bringing the sailors on board to know Christ. In the end, 125 sailors came to know the Lord before the ship sank at Pearl Harbor!

Nothing in the world is so satisfying as leading a person to know Christ. Maybe it is because it is a task of eternal significance. All other tasks have only temporary impact. Just think of a person being saved from eternal punishment. Just think of a person enjoying eternal life with us forever.

There is a story of what it's like in heaven, when a person dies. In this story the person who dies is greeted at heaven's gate by the person who led him to Christ. The saddest people are the people whose names are never called to greet a newcomer to heaven. While this is only a story, its meaning is clear. We can take nothing out of this world, but we can bring souls into heaven's eternity through Christ. For that we rejoice.

Before Christ ascended into heaven, he commanded us to go and teach all people about him. He promised he would always be with us. There is a lady named Louise, who is not afraid to follow Christ's command and share her faith. Not long ago she sat in the hospital waiting room of a small town in Alberta, Canada. She noticed a man who had just recovered from a heart attack. She asked him, if he would have died would he have gone to heaven? The man did not think so. He had been a Catholic in name only for years, but he did not know how to be saved. Louise shared with him the gospel for about ten minutes, and then he prayed with her a prayer, thanking God for his salvation and commiting his life to Jesus. He had tears in his eyes and he said he would carry the seed of faith back home with him to eastern Canada. What a gratifying experience! In a short span of fifteen minutes, Louise had helped one person to escape eternal death.

James 5:20 reads: "Whoever turns a sinner from the error of his way will save him from death."

Prayer:

Dear God, fill me with the desire to do your work, the work of bringing people to know you and be saved. Help me see the immediate need for people to know you before they die. Send your Holy Spirit to guide me and those to whom I witness. Make me bold and help me lead many people to your righteousness. Amen.

Make My Life an Alleluia!

Really Clean

Psalm 103:1-12

Praise the LORD, O my soul; all my inmost being, praise his holy name. Praise the LORD, O my soul, and forget not all his benefits—who forgives all your sins and heals all your diseases, who redeems your life from the pit and crowns you with love and compassion, who satisfies your desires with good things so that your youth is renewed like the eagle's. The LORD works righteousness and justice for all the oppressed. He made known his ways to Moses, his deeds to the people of Israel: The LORD is compassionate and gracious, slow to anger, abounding in love. He will not always accuse, nor will he harbor his anger forever; he does not treat us as our sins deserve or repay us according to our iniquities. For as high as the heavens are above the earth, so great is his love for those who fear him; as far as the east is from the west, so far has he removed our transgressions from us.

Erma Bombeck has funny commentaries on what it is like to be a housewife. One of her funnier quotes is: "Housework, if done right, can kill you." This strikes me as humorous because there is some truth to the saying. On days when I feverishly try to clean the whole house, I am literally exhausted. But some of the time I am in too much of a hurry to do a thorough job. If company is coming in an hour, I skip over the crumbs and dust hiding on the kitchen floor under the hot water registers. The floor gets washed but not waxed, and the top shelves of the livingroom bookshelf do not get dusted. But outwardly the house looks

How not to get rid of sin. . . .

Soap and Water

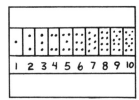
Rationalize

Cover up

Compare sins

Punish oneself

Try to improve

How to get rid of sin. . . .

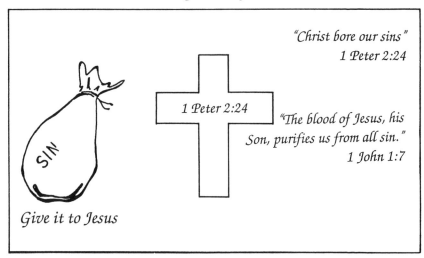

Give it to Jesus

"Christ bore our sins"
1 Peter 2:24

1 Peter 2:24

"The blood of Jesus, his Son, purifies us from all sin."
1 John 1:7

pretty good to any casual visitor. Still, I know the house could be cleaner!

Once when I was about ten years old, my sister and I were hurrying to finish the dishes before the company came. We didn't quite finish, so, as the company drove up, we hid the dirty kettles in the clothes hamper and dryer, and wiped the counter. It looked neat when the company came, but we knew better. (It was good no one turned on the dryer!)

If we compare dirt to sins, we may realize that our lives are pretty dirty, even if much is hidden to the eye. It is impossible to somehow scrub away this grime of sin by ourselves. Only Jesus can do that. 1 John 1:7-9 reads: "But if we walk in the light, as he is in the light, we have fellowship with one another, and the blood of Jesus, his Son, purifies us from all sin. If we claim to be without sin, we deceive ourselves and the truth is not in us. If we confess our sins, he is faithful and just and will forgive us our sins and purify us from all unrighteousness."

Before it was finally outlawed by the government, American Indians used mutilation or self-torture as a means to atone for their sins. That may seem primitive and even senseless, but think of how people in our society today attempt to atone for their own sins. Some people attempt to redo things they have done wrong, trying to do them better the second time. Some people try to do a large number of good deeds to make up for the bad deeds they have done. Others try meticulously to remember every sin they have done in order to repent of it and make themselves right before God by the arduous task of confession. Still others may try to get so busy and tired out that they forget their sins, "covering" them up with a lot of activity.

Have you ever tried to pick out exactly what you have said or done wrong in an argument? It can be very complicated trying to figure out what you said wrong, whom you hurt, what you have to forgive, what you should have said but didn't. As the psalmist cried out, "Who can discern his errors? Forgive my hidden faults" (Psalm 19:12).

We can leave the job of scrubbing away and cleaning up our sins to God. Only he can do it with the suffering, bleeding and death of his precious Son. Only he can do it, because he alone does a thorough job. He understands all of our sins. He knows what wrongs we have said, thought or done. He knows when we failed to do the good things he wants us to do. He alone can cleanse us from these hidden faults.

"Praise the Lord, O my soul; all my inmost being, praise his holy name. Praise the Lord, O my soul, and forget not all his benefits—who forgives all your sins and heals all your diseases."

Prayer:

Dear Jesus, if I could only touch the hem of your garment, I would be well. Help me reach out to you with the hands of faith to grasp your redeeming work for me. Heal me spiritually so that I may be cleansed from work-righteousness. Help me cling to you alone in faith and let go of everything else I try to do to make myself look good in your eyes. Cleanse me, Jesus. I praise your name! Amen.

Make My Life an Alleluia!

The Little Things Mean So Much

Matthew 10:40, 42
"He who receives you receives me. . . .And if anyone gives even a cup of cold water to one of these little ones because he is my disciple, I tell you the truth, he will certainly not lose his reward."

How important are those little things, those seemingly unimportant things, we do as wives and mothers every day: making meals, washing dishes, changing diapers, sweeping the floor, changing the toilet paper roll, giving that last drink of water at bedtime? I know that these things can get mighty boring. Have you ever noticed all the havoc that occurs if they are not done, and how much more smoothly things go if they are done? Jesus puts a high priority on a task such as giving a drink of water to a little child. It is like we were giving it to the Lord himself.

Those little things do mean a lot! One Saturday morning I had talked to a young mother about all of her troubles and I felt emotionally drained. At noon my husband came home from the grocery store with a big box of chocolates just for me. "Thanks! I needed that!" I thought as I hugged him.

We all need to feel God's abundant love and care, and God gives us to each other in families to share love and care. My husband is really happy when I make homemade chili. In fact, he heats some up for breakfast and lunch, because it makes him feel warm and loved.

One day I made an impromptu fruit basket (mainly bananas) for one of our needy families at church. Later they sent me a card, explaining that during that particular week they had a lot of car repairs and no money to buy fruit. They loved the fruit, especially the bananas!

Another time I sent a "care" package of Christian bookmarks, gifts and artificial flowers to a friend of mine going through a seperation. She said the package arrived after one of her lowest days, and that it was as if someone had heaped love on her. She in turn read the Bible verses enclosed in the package to her aunt, whose husband was dying of cancer. Her aunt was also uplifted! What a chain reaction.

A pastor's wife baked a beautiful, heart-shaped anniversary cake for the grandparents of her son's girlfriend. The grandparents had company over, and they all "oohed and ahhed" about the wonderful treat and how thoughtful it had been for that woman to take the time to make such a surprise for them. That little deed of love went a long way to show that God indeed cares for his children.

Often we need to get ideas from others on how to be messengers of God's love. . .the thoughtful card or letter, the bouquet of real or silk flowers, the telephone call during an illness, the hospital visit, the gift to a prisoner, the Bible sent to a friend, the invitation to a ladies' group at church, a special cake for one's child written with "I love you, Johnny," the pretty way the house looks when guests arrive, the favorite dish for hubby.

Prayer:

God, thank you for taking such *good* care of me—protecting me, giving me forgiveness and eternal life and many surprise blessings. Please pop ideas into my head about how I can surprise others so that they may know your loving care. Amen.

Let Your Light So Shine

Matthew 5:14-16
"You are the light of the world. A city on a hill cannot be hidden. Neither do people light a lamp and put it under a bowl. Instead they put it on its stand, and it gives light to everyone in the house. In the same way, let your light shine before men, that they may see your good deeds and praise your Father in heaven."

The highest compliment I have ever received came from a girlfriend whom I had helped spiritually, emotionally and physically through some very rough times. She said, "I can see the glory of God through your shining example." To have people see God in my actions and not me is my goal. How many things must one person do for another before the truth that God indeed loves them comes alive? There are many things we can do for our families, friends, people at work, new visitors to our churches. Here is a brief list:

1. Witness to them about the love of Christ and how God has been active in your life.
2. Give them Bibles, religious bookmarks, letters, birth day cards, flowers, pies, cookies, hot dishes.
3. Visit them in the hospital or resthome.
4. Talk with them, being a good listener.
5. Share a joke.
6. Decorate a special cake for them.
7. Surprise them with a birthday party, baby shower, congratulations party for any reason.
8. Take them on a picnic.
9. Go swimming, hiking, biking with them.
10. Have them over for supper.

11. Give them food from your pantry or garden.
12. Give them a hug.
13. Compliment them sincerely.
14. Encourage them.
15. Greet them with kind words.
16. Smile.
17. Remember details about the conversations you've had with them.
18. Pray for them and with them.
19. Sing hymns with them.
20. Read the Bible to them.
21. Do craft projects with them.
22. Tell them that God loves them very much!
23. Invite them to go with you to church or a meeting for fellowship with other Christians.

I like to make cakes, especially for my children on special occasions. Remember Alice, the maid on the Brady Bunch? She was always ready with an appropriately decorated cake. One episode showed her making two cakes to be ready for any outcome of the football game. One read, "Congratulations, Champs," and one read "Better luck next time!"

Recently I made a cake for my twelve year old, the second oldest of our five children. It read, "We love you, Seth." I told him I thought he needed a cake like that. I asked him if I was right. "Yup," he agreed.

Everyone needs that extra hug, that smile, that compliment, that pat on the shoulder. But we're not just making people feel good. We are drawing their attention to the unending source of love we find in Jesus our Lord. May God bless all of our deeds of love to his glory!

Prayer:
Dear Jesus, help my light to shine before men, women and children, that people everywhere may glorify you. Amen.

A Lesson on Hands

Psalm 73:23-28
Yet I am always with you; you hold me by my right hand. You guide me with your counsel, and afterward you will take me into glory. Whom have I in heaven but you? And earth has nothing I desire besides you. My flesh and my heart may fail, but God is the strength of my heart and my portion forever. Those who are far from you will perish; you destroy all who are unfaithful to you. But as for me, it is good to be near God. I have made the Sovereign LORD my refuge; I will tell of all your deeds.

I fell asleep at 10:30 p.m. at the kitchen table on a cold winter night. When I awoke it was 12:30 a.m. My first thought was how quickly time must pass from the moment of death to the resurrection of the body. My hands were numb from leaning on them, but as I moved them, blood rushed back to revive them, reminding me of the new life I had received at my baptism. As I got ready for bed, I noticed that my hands were cold. I remembered that many times God had warmed me with his love. Isaiah 41:10 states: "I will strengthen you and help you; I will uphold you with my righteous right hand." God had promised and God had faithfully held my hand in the past.

As I washed my hands, they hurt because the cold weather had made them chapped. I thought of the nail-pierced hands that had bought my forgiveness. I rubbed on some hand cream and thought of the many times throughout my life that God had healed my hands.

Then I went to bed and folded my hands. I thanked God for the privilege of prayer and for my lesson on hands.

Prayer:
Dear Lord, I give myself to you. "Take my life and let it be consecrated, Lord, to thee. Take my moments and my days. Let them flow in ceaseless praise! Take my hands and let them move at the impulse of thy love. Take my feet and let them be swift and beautiful for thee." Amen.

Joy to the World

Luke 2:10-12
But the angel said to them, "Do not be afraid. I bring you good news of great joy that will be for all the people. Today in the town of David a Savior has been born to you; he is Christ the Lord. This will be a sign to you: You will find a baby wrapped in cloths and lying in a manger."

One of the pleasures of living near Edmonton, Alberta is the opportunity to shop at the vast West Edmonton Mall, reported to be the largest indoor shopping mall in the world. While doing some Christmas shopping there, I heard the beautiful, piped-in Christmas carols. The message of these carols was the true meaning of Christmas, but I wondered how many shoppers heard or understood the words. Most of the shoppers seemed in a dither to check price tags and buy items on their lists.

One of the carols played was "Joy to the World." I wondered how many people all over the world actually knew the impact of the angel's message that first Christmas night. Think for a minute about all the people in your relation, in your town, in your country, in the world. The angel had good news of great joy for all the people of the whole world! "The Lord is come!"

"Let earth receive her King," the song continues. The King of kings is Jesus Christ. Many people set up other kings in their lives such as money, success, recognition, fame, sex or power. But Jesus is the real King. Born in poverty and meekness, and bearing the sin of all by suffering and dying on a cruel cross, our glorious and victorious risen Savior and Lord now reigns in unapproachable light in heaven. To Jesus, our Servant and King, belong all the praise and glory now and forever and ever!

The next line of the hymn reads, "Let every heart prepare Him room." That means we have to sweep away some things out of our heart so there is room. With God's help we can sweep away the dirt of our sins of pride, greed, jealousy, cynicism, anger, worry, doubts, grudges, slothfulness, lust. Our hearts can be clean through the blood of Jesus, shed for the forgiveness of our sins. Then Jesus can set up his throne in our hearts, and oh, the joy and peace that flood into our hearts when Jesus reigns as King there!

"And heaven and nature sing." I imagine that the angels sing louder and more beautifully at Christmas time than any other time in the year. How happy God must be to look down and hear his people singing carols for his Son's birth. But the message of joy is for the *whole world.* We must go out and tell others the good news, one by one, so that the whole world can join in singing praises to the King of kings. Joy to the WORLD!

Prayer:
Dear God, thank you for sending Jesus to bring joy to the whole world. Forgive my sins. Fill me with your unending joy that I may share this joy with my family, my friends, my town, my country and with the whole world. Amen.

Resting in God

Numbers 6:24-26
"The LORD bless you and keep you; the LORD make his face shine upon you and be gracious to you; the LORD turn his face toward you and give you peace."

"Nothing is impossible with God," the angel Gabriel said to Mary, when Mary asked how she could bear a son, since she was a virgin. How often have you seen God's power displayed so plainly in your life? Many times I have been in the depths of doubts, wondering if I had any faith at all. Then I have prayed for an answer to my doubts, and God has faithfully supplied all that I need. God has repeatedly pulled my feet out of the net and set me on the path of life. With God nothing is impossible.

It is in those glowing times, especially on Sundays after hearing his Word and receiving his Holy Supper, that I feel thankful to God and have a glimpse of what it means to rest in God. I can't think of anything more pleasant than to end a worshipful day with an evening visit with Christian friends. The food, the fun, the laughter, the freedom from worries or cares, is almost heavenly. One feels such inexpressible joy at those times, such irrepressible peace and rest, such lingering happiness. That, coupled with the gifts of children and the joys of married life, makes one feel full of God's love and full of gratitude to God, the Giver of all good gifts. The sweetest days are those spent resting in God's love, and praising Him constantly without words, with only the continuous joy springing from one's heart to his throne on high.

One basks in the sunshine of God's love in those pure, heavenly times. But what about all the other days—the humdrum ones? With the continual sacrifice of praise to God on our lips, humdrum days can become happy days. Each day can be new and joyful no matter what is happening. God created us to enjoy the new life that he alone gives and to praise Him with our whole heart. In Psalm 22 the writer describes God as being enthroned on the praises of Israel. God lives within the praises of his people. When we praise God, the enemy flees because the enemy cannot stand our praises to the Lord. God fills us with his joy and love as we praise him. The more joy we have, the more spontaneous our praises. The more we show praise, the more God smiles. He loves to see us happy and thankful.

Prayer:
Dear Jesus, I praise you for always lifting me out of doubts and low times in my life. I praise you for giving me new life through your death for my sins and your victorious rising to life. I praise you in joy! Amen.

The Praise Cake

Philippians 4:4
Rejoice in the Lord always. I will say it again: Rejoice!

A couple of years ago, I frosted a cake and wrote on it with big letters, "PRAISE GOD!" I set the cake on a lazy susan with hooks for cups underneath. From the cup handles I hung cards, noting the things for which we could praise God. Some of the cards read, "For the new fish," "For an 'A' on the science test," "For no cavities at the dentist," "For a safe trip to the farm," "For the way the house didn't burn down when we left for three hours and P. J. (our three-year-old) put two pancakes in the toaster oven at 400 degrees!"

It is pleasant to think of reasons to praise God. Recently, for example, a friend and I traveled to a hospital thirty miles away from home to visit a dying man. As we completed the last mile of our journey, I noticed we were out of gas. I had *just* enough gas left in the car to pull into a nearby gas station. Praise God! He took care of us and allowed us to get safely out of the heavy city traffic and close enough to a gas station.

In the famous writing entitled "Desiderata" the author says, "Many fears are born of fatigue and loneliness." I have noticed this about my life. It is easier to be fearful and harder to praise God when I am tired. And it is helpful to have the fellowship and prayers of fellow Christians to buoy up my spiritual life of praise when I am lonely.

In the movie "Pollyanna" the star played the "Glad Game." The idea of the game was to think of as many things as one could for which to be thankful. We can be thankful for how God works out the little details of our lives. One night I was making a poster for our church prayer chain. The poster was to be displayed in church the next day. It was late and I was trying to think of the reference to the passage, "With God all things are possible." I happened to glance at a friend's card and on it was the Bible reference, Matthew 19:26. My friend never wrote out a passage because she wanted the person receiving the card to open the Bible and keep on reading. I was astonished when I looked up Matthew 19:26. It read, ". . .with God all things are possible." I praised God for his providence!

Prayer:
"I will extol the LORD at all times; his praise will always be on my lips. My soul will boast in the LORD; let the afflicted hear and rejoice. Glorify the LORD with me; let us exalt his name together" (Psalm 34:1-3). I praise you, God! Amen.

The Laughter Chapter

Proverbs 17:22
A cheerful heart is good medicine, but a crushed spirit dries up the bones.

Physicians have found that laughter is therapeutic. Christians can be free to laugh and be merry because God is their refuge and Savior from the storms of life. It is fun to tell jokes, laugh and not take life so seriously. God gives us laughter as a special gift from him. He gives us good friends. Every good and perfect gift is from above, coming down from the Father. Christians can relax, knowing their eternal destiny is secure and their present existence is in God's hands. Permit me to share some laughter with you from my house:

I asked my husband one Valentine's Day, "Honey, did you really mean all those wonderful things on the card you gave me?" He replied glibly, "Oh, at least fifty percent."

Question: "How many days of the week begin with 'T'?"
Answer: "Two—today and tomorrow."

Question: "How many seconds in the year?"
Answer: "12. January 2, February 2, March 2, etc."

Minister: "If you have three dollars, and you want to save it in this broken cup and give one-tenth to the church, what will you have left at the end of the week?"
Child: "A broken cup."

A boy scout troop got lost in the woods: As they had been instructed in case of an emergency, they fired three shots into the air and waited. Nothing happened. They fired three more shots, but then they ran out of arrows, so they had to wait to be rescued.

My son, age 6, showing me his schoolwork: "Look, Mom, all goods and smiley faces and no backwards fives!"

Hans, Peter and their mother were climbing in the Alps. All at once Hans lost his footing and fell off the side of the mountain. Peter immediately alerted his mother, "Look, Ma, no Hans!"

"The Moist Dinner" or "The Best Laid Plans":

My husband had been complaining for a week that I hadn't been putting much thought into meals. I had been awfully busy, so I thought that on Friday night I would make a fancy dinner to kind of get back into his good graces again and to save our marriage from discontent. I prepared a beautiful lasagna meal, complete with wine, good china, a tablecloth and dessert.

My husband thought he would fix a small leak in the bathtub faucet before he sat down to eat. He felt that any drip, however small, should be remedied to save money. As I began to eat with the kids, suddenly I heard loud shouting from the bathroom. The small leak could not be fixed, and the faucet could not be replaced on the stem, so *hot* water was now gushing out of the faucet. Worse yet, the shut-off valve was broken, and the great flood of water gushed out and over the tub for twenty minutes, while the kids and Steve bailed with buckets as fast as they could. The neighbors came out wondering why we were watering our front lawn with buckets of hot water. Finally, we called a repairman who turned off the ground water. An hour later Steve sat down to eat. His comment was, "It was a lovely meal, Dear!"

Prayer:
Dear God, thank you for giving us friends, fun and good times. Help us to laugh, have fun and enjoy the good life you have given us. Thank you for the security we have in the redeeming work of your Son, Jesus Christ. Amen.

Speak to One Another with Psalms

Ephesians 5:18-20
Do not get drunk on wine, which leads to debauchery. Instead, be filled with the Spirit. Speak to one another with psalms, hymns and spiritual songs. Sing and make music in your heart to the Lord, always giving thanks to God the Father for everything, in the name of our Lord Jesus Christ.

Do you ever feel depressed because there are words spoken in your house that you know shouldn't be spoken, e.g., fighting, angry words, put-downs, bad language? Sometimes children are sent to their rooms to cool down. Adults later come back and say, "I'm sorry I got angry." Lack of sleep can contribute to irritability, and sometimes a bad habit has to be broken by first realizing it is a sin and then praying about it. But there are also ways to prevent flare-ups. For example, by trying to keep everyone well fed, by giving each one attention, by filling the house with Christian songs on tape or record, by singing songs of praise softly, by speaking to each other about what God has done in our lives.

An example of speaking to each other about what God has done occurred in the car one wintry evening. My three boys—ages eleven, six and four—and I were driving on the freeway to our destination ten minutes away, when I realized we were almost out of gas. I quickly turned off the freeway and explored dark, unfamiliar city streets looking for a gas station. At one point I turned a corner into a one-way street, going the wrong way! All the cars' headlights were facing us at the stop light as we quickly made a U-turn and got out of there. After driving around some more, I said, "Boys, just pray!"

We prayed together, "Dear God, help us to find a gas station." It wasn't long before we found one. A wild looking gas attendant filled our tank, and we were on the road again.

We still didn't know how to get to our destination. A thought came to me, "Pray first!" It was easier to pray aloud again. "Dear God, help us get there."

My son added, "And help us not to run out of gas again."

Soon the way was clear. It had been a Spirit-filled trip. We thanked God for keeping us safe.

Prayer:
Dear God, fill my family and me with your Holy Spirit and help us to speak to one another of your constant love. Amen.

Trust Level

Luke 2:20
The shepherds returned, glorifying and praising God for all the things they had heard and seen, which were just as they had been told.

Have you ever noticed that your children's trust level grows everytime you tell them something is going to happen, and then it occurs? For example, I might tell them that certain people are coming over at 6:00 p.m. for supper at our house. When these people come, they know Mom was telling the truth. Or I might say, "We are going ice-skating tonight." When we get in the car and go to the rink, the children know that Mom keeps her promises.

In the above text, the shepherds had just seen the baby Jesus. Everything was just as they had been told. When we get to heaven we will be able to see how wonderful everything is there. It will be just as we have been told. God has built our trust level too. First, he promised a Savior, and Jesus was born. God promised that he would place on Jesus the sin of us all (Isaiah 53), and he did. "Christ died for our sins according to the Scriptures" (1 Corinthians 15:3). God the Father raised Christ from the dead to show he was satisfied with Christ's sacrifice. In John 2:19 Jesus promised, "Destroy this temple, and I will raise it again in three days." By his victorious resurrection Jesus fulfilled this promise.

Jesus promised always to be with us and send us the Holy Spirit. We know from the peace, joy, love and blessings God has given us that he is indeed with us.

Jesus promised to return again in glory with all his holy angels. We trust that he will return, but we don't know when. In the meantime our trust level grows, as we pray for the Holy Spirit's guidance, and God supplies that guidance, just as he promised.

Prayer:
Come, Lord Jesus! Return soon! In the meantime, continue to build my trust level. Amen.

Jesus Loves You, Mommy

Proverbs 22: 6
Train a child in the way he should go, and when he is old he will not turn from it.

It had been a long night. We couldn't decide whether or not to take our four-year-old P. J. to the hospital. He had been breathing rapidly (about 50 times per minute) all night, but seemed to be resting comfortably.

We weren't sure if it was asthma or a reaction to allergy. P. J. coughed a lot that night and in the morning seemed much better after a drink of hot cocoa. P .J. and I sat at the kitchen table reading the account of the feeding of the 5,000 from his Sunday School leaflet. Then we talked about how Jesus takes care of us, and I said a prayer, "Dear Jesus, please make P. J. better." As we were going upstairs, I coughed twice. Immediately P. J. stopped on a step, folded his little hands and said, "Dear God, make Mommy better. Amen."

One of the most gratifying blessings is to see God's

Holy Spirit, present at our children's baptism, at work in their speech and actions. When we witness to our children, the Holy Spirit works in their hearts. We are training our children in the way of eternal life. One of the greatest joys is to see them witness back to us.

One day P. J. noticed I looked sad. He hugged me and said, "Jesus loves you, Mommy." Another day my son Micah, age seven, was listening to us talk about what would happen if the plane I planned to take would crash. "God will help you, Mommy," Micah said.

My daughter Mary was nine when she said, "It would be a wonderful Christmas, even if we didn't get any presents, because Jesus is here."

One of our children needed a special medicine every night for two months. It had been a long, tiring day, and I didn't feel like giving the medicine that night. Two of my children came into the room singing "The Joy of the Lord Is My Strength." Immediately my spirits revived, and I had strength from the Lord.

Prayer:
Dear Lord, please help me to train up my children in the way that leads to eternal life. Make all the other demands for my time pale by insignificance. Thank you for giving me my children. Amen.

The Worry List

Peter 5:7
Cast all your anxiety on him because he cares for you.

On Monday of one week I wrote down all my worries. On Tuesday I read the list over. On Wednesday I worried some more. On Thursday I worried some more. On Friday I longed to be free of worries. On Saturday I wondered if I ever would be. On Sunday I went to church and praised God in the choir. On Sunday afternoon I sang with a mass choir of eighty voices, practicing songs of praise for the Reformation festival. On Sunday evening I sang with the choir at the joyful installation of a new pastor at our church.

On Monday I looked at my worry list and laughed. Every single item on the worry list had evaporated in the sunshine of praises to God. Augustine said long ago, "Oh, thou, who madest us for thee, we have no rest until we rest in thee." I like to say it this way: "Human beings were created to praise God. Unless they are doing exactly that, they are not happy."

Our Bible verse encourages us to cast our worries

on God. God knows all our worries, cares and doubts even before we share them with him in prayer. Remember what Jesus said in the Gospel of Matthew: "Are not two sparrows sold for a penny? Yet not one of them will fall to the ground apart from the will of your Father. And even the very hairs of your head are all numbered. So don't be afraid; you are worth more than many sparrows" (Matthew 10:29-31).

If God knows how many hairs we have on our head, then he also knows how many pimples we have on our face, how many aches we have in our body, how many doubts or worries we have in our head. All we need to do is draw near to him in praise and thank him for how he is going to lift us up above all these problems. One of the psalmists exclaimed how God inhabits the praises of his people. When we are praising God, doing the very purpose for which we were created, God is present to help and cheer us and smile upon us as we put our trust in him.

Prayer:
O Lord God, you who inhabit the praises of your people, open our mouths to sing your praises. Lift us up to praise your holy name and to see Jesus seated at the right hand of your glory in heaven. We thank and praise you, God, for making every doubt, worry and trial in our lives work out for your glory. Amen.

Fitting into God's Plan

Isaiah 55:9-11
As the heavens are higher than the earth, so are my ways higher than your ways and my thoughts than your thoughts. As the rain and the snow come down from heaven, and do not return to it without watering the earth and making it bud and flourish, so that it yields seed for the sower and bread for the eater, so is my word that goes out from my mouth: It will not return to me empty, but will accomplish what I desire and achieve the purpose for which I sent it.

Think of how high the heavens are above the earth. Just think of how much higher God's thoughts are than ours! Yet God chooses us humans to fit into his divine plan for the salvation of people on this earth.

While making evangelism calls one evening we stopped at the home of a woman whose husband was gravely ill. We had tried to visit her earlier in the evening, but she was not home. We drove past the house again and were happy to find her home. We talked and prayed together. The next day she confided in me that she had been feeling very depressed and that it was as if God had sent us to her that evening. We had fit into God's plan.

A young woman in our choir was ill and waiting for the doctor's prognosis. For choir devotions she read Psalm 121:

> I lift up my eyes to the hills—where does my help come from? My help comes from the Lord, the Maker of heaven and earth. He will not let your foot slip—he who watches over you will not slumber; indeed, he who watches over Israel will neither slumber not sleep. The Lord watches over you—the Lord is your shade at your right hand; the sun will not harm you by day, nor the moon by night. The Lord will keep you from all harm—he will watch over your life; the Lord will watch over your coming and going

both now and forevermore (Psalm 121:1-8).

The message of this psalm spoke to her as she waited to find out the seriousness of her illness. The same message spoke to me as God erased thoughts from a bad movie I had seen the day before. I was assured that God is just and does punish the wicked, preserving his own from all harm. God's word had accomplished its purpose.

Not long ago an evangelism team in Texas was having trouble finding the address for a call. As they knocked on the door of a house with the right number, a lady across the street yelled, "They're not home, but they'll be back later." The team thanked her and then noticed that she had been crying. They asked if she would like to talk with someone. The lady explained that her husband had told her that they had to get divorced.

Soon the husband came home. Seeing the three callers in suits and ties, he assumed that they were the divorce lawyers. After explaining who they were, the callers found out that the man really didn't want a divorce, but he had lost his job and thought that divorce was the only way out. The callers shared the good news that Christ has freed us from our sins through his death on the cross. We have forgiveness and we can forgive. Soon the couple were hugging each other and crying. The evangelism callers quietly left, praising God for leading them to that house. Back in the car they checked again for the address they wanted to find. As it turned out, they had knocked on the door of a house a whole block away from the correct address!

God faithfully makes sure that his word goes out and waters the parched ground of people's hearts, making them bud and flourish.

Prayer:
Dear God, I praise you for helping me fit into your plan to save all people. Keep me watchful for opportunities to share your word. Amen.

His Mercy Endures Forever

Psalm 96:1-3
Sing to the LORD a new song; sing to the LORD, all the earth. Sing to the LORD, praise his name; proclaim his salvation day after day. Declare his glory among the nations, his marvelous deeds among all peoples.

When we moved to Canada we had the pleasure of renting a home from a lovely Christian couple, Mr. and Mrs. B. Their generosity reminded us over and over of God's constant love. The very night we moved into our home, the couple had us over for dinner, even though they were busy unpacking from their move a couple of days before. As we began putting things away in our new home, we noticed that Mr. and Mrs. B. had cleaned our home to perfection, with not even a speck of dust on a hat rack. They also brought us fresh garden produce and two dozen eggs.

The second week we were there, Mrs. B. invited me to a lovely luncheon and paid my way. We were given apples from their orchard, and Mrs. B. even came over to help me can the apple juice. After that, followed many invitations to come over for tea. Mrs. B. was a most gracious hostess and usually sent along a bag of homemade cookies when I left for home.

One evening Mr. B. surprised us with a special treat. It was the evening I had burned the whole supper—meat, potatoes and corn. Mr. B. rang the door bell and presented us with a piping hot homemade apple pie. The pie saved the day! Truly it was a blessing to know these people. They even remembered us in their prayers.

God's love is even more wonderful than that of Mr. and Mrs. B. God created a beautiful world for us to enjoy, but that's not all God did. God sent Jesus to die for our sins, so we could be completely forgiven. Jesus, God's Son, showed His power over death by raising himself from the dead. God removed the power of death. But there's more. God promised to be with us always. God promised his Holy Spirit to help us along the way. God has promised to answer all of our prayers. Jesus even prays for us! God promised us the gift of eternal life. Heaven and all of its joy and peace are still ahead. Think of how many blessings God has already given you and how many surprises lie ahead in this life and in heaven forever with HIM. God's love endures forever!

Prayer:

The Lord is my shepherd, I shall not be in want. He makes me lie down in green pastures, he leads me beside quiet waters, he restores my soul. He guides me in paths of righteousness for his name's sake. Even though I walk through the valley of the shadow of death, I will fear no evil, for you are with me; your rod and your staff, they comfort me. You prepare a table before me in the presence of my enemies. You annoint my head with oil; my cup overflows. Surely goodness and love will follow me all the days of my life, and I will dwell in the house of the Lord forever (Psalm 23). Amen.

His Eye Is on the Sparrow

Matthew 10:29-31
Are not two sparrows sold for a penny? Yet not one of them will fall to the ground apart from the will of your Father. And even the very hairs of your head are all numbered. So don't be afraid; you are worth more than many sparrows.

It was one of those "blah" days. Everything seemed humdrum. My husband was preaching at another church that morning; so I had the two little boys, ages two and five, and he had the three older children. As we drove down the familiar road to church, I stopped the car to allow a mother duck and her ducklings to cross. "How cute," I thought. Little did I know that this was my object lesson for the day. As we left church, I remember thinking that it was not one of the more inspiring services I had ever attended. I definitely felt humdrum!

As we arrived home, I put the car into park in front of the garage door, left the motor running, and stepped out to open the door. As I approached the car door to step back in, I realized to my terror that the car was slowly moving forward! My two-year-old had pushed the shift lever into drive.

In a split second I pictured, in slow motion, the whole front of the garage caving in.

I screamed in fright, and my two-year-old figured he had done something wrong and pushed the lever into reverse. Slowly the car rolled backwards. I swung open the car door and tried to jump in, but just then the car picked up speed on the incline. I slammed the car door shut and noticed the look of pure terror on the faces of my two little boys. The car rolled faster down the driveway and across the street. The hill on the neighbor's lawn across the street stopped the car suddenly, with the rear of the car up in the air and the headlights in the street.

My knees were like jelly as I got into the car and drove it forward into the garage. No one was hurt! God had cared for my boys and me, just as he had cared for the mother duck and her ducklings. I praised God for his constant protection.

Prayer:
Dear Heavenly Father, thank you for always protecting my family and me from all danger. Please continue to be with me, and help me constantly to praise you for taking care of me. Amen.

The Best Part

John 3:16
"For God so loved the world that he gave his one and only Son, that whoever believes in him shall not perish but have eternal life."

I was on my hands and knees outlining letters on a large banner for the Sunday School program. "What does that say?" my youngest, P. J., asked.

"It says, 'Jesus died for all and rose again. Heaven is ours!'" I replied.

P. J. thought for a minute. "Heaven is ours. That's the best part!" he said.

Christians look forward to heaven. I found that older people in the rest home where I visited weekly, really longed for their heavenly home. Hilda, an elderly lady with shaky hands and thick wire-rimmed glasses, sat in her wheelchair and mused, "I dreamed I went to heaven and saw Jesus and the angels. Jesus called my name." Hilda was gray and pale, and her body was wasting away, but her eyes were alive with hope. She was looking forward to eternal life. She spoke again, "I was in such pain when I was sick. I felt all choked up in my stomach and I lost thirty pounds. In heaven there won't be any pain."

Hilda was not the only older person looking forward to heaven. Florence, at ninety-one years, told me confidently, "If you don't see me the next time you come for the hymn sing, you'll know that I have gone to heaven."

Jesus has promised that in heaven there will be no pain, that God will wipe away every tear from our eyes, that God will be with us, his people, forever and ever. Jesus went to prepare a place for us, and he will come back to take us to be with him. What joy that day will bring!

I remember on Sunday drives, when we were small, my mother showed us beautiful sunsets. She told us maybe that is how beautiful heaven will be. Heaven will indeed be beautiful, as the book of Revelation describes. But the best part will be that Jesus is there, and we will at last be safe at home.

Prayer:

Let me be Thine forever,
Thou faithful God and Lord;
Let me forsake Thee never
Nor wander from Thy Word.
Lord, do not let me waver,
But give me steadfastness,
And for such grace forever
Thy holy name I'll bless.

Lord Jesus, my Salvation,
My Light, my Life divine,
My only Consolation,
Oh, make me wholly Thine!
For Thou hast dearly bought me
With blood and bitter pain.
Let me, since Thou hast sought me,
Eternal life obtain.

And Thou, O Holy Spirit,
My Comforter and Guide,
Grant that in Jesus' merit
I always may confide,
Him to the end confessing
Whom I have known by faith.
Give me Thy constant blessing
And grant a Christian death.   Amen.

My Dream

Matthew 13:40-43
"As the weeds are pulled up and burned in the fire, so it will be at the end of the age. The Son of Man will send out his angels, and they will weed out of his kingdom everything that causes sin and all who do evil. They will throw them into the fiery furnace, where there will be weeping and gnashing of teeth. Then the righteous will shine like the sun in the kingdom of their Father. He who has ears, let him hear."

One night I had an exciting dream, which I remembered in detail and labeled: "Shoot-out at the Cathedral." The dream was about World War III. Christians had been worshiping in a large cathedral, as the explosive sounds of gunfire and bombs drew closer. The enemy troops were advancing into the church. I was talking with a newcomer to our church. Time was running out. The first shot inside the cathedral pierced the silence. People scurried in all directions to escape the rapid gunfire. I yelled to the people and my new friend, "Jesus died for you!"

"Died for you! Died for you!" the huge cathedral echoed back.

"And rose again!" I yelled.

"And rose again! And rose again!" the echoes rang out, fading into space.

I was ready. The time had run out. There was no escape unless I were to play dead. I went up to the altar to lie down and play dead, knowing that they could still discover me and kill me.

Dreams can be frightening at times. I was glad that my dream had a happy ending. I was ready to die because I had found my escape plan in Jesus. Even in my subconscious, I knew the way out of impending doom. Jesus, in the above text, warns us of the terrors and punishment for the ungodly. But Jesus continues to assure us that the righteous will shine like the sun in the kingdom of their Father. Jesus has made it possible for us to shine throughout eternity because of his death for our sins, his shedding of blood on the cross and his glorious resurrection.

Not long ago I had the privilege of playing the piano for a rest home sing-a-long. One of the favorite hymns played was "Amazing Grace." The elderly people, many of them shaky and with poor eyesight, sang out the words from memory: "When we've been there ten thousand years, bright shining as the sun, we've no less days to sing God's praise than when we'd first begun." At that moment the afternoon sun flooded the room with a brilliant light. I played a little louder on the piano and thanked God that one day we would shine like the sun in the kingdom of our Father.

Prayer:
Dear God, thank you for providing me with an escape from eternal death through Jesus our Lord. Make me ready and help me to get other people ready for the day when time on this earth runs out. Thank you, God. Amen.

Overflowing with Praise!

I Timothy 6:17
Command those who are rich in this present world not to be arrogant nor to put their hope in wealth, which is so uncertain, but to put their hope in God, who richly provides us with everything for our enjoyment.

During my weekly visits to a rest home in Stony Plain, Alberta, I met a charming ninety-one-year-old lady named Florence. I met her briefly in the hallway after our hymn sing. I asked her if she had any children. She replied that she had one child still living and two up in heaven waiting for her. She went on to tell me that Jesus was her Savior and that she witnessed for him every opportunity she had. Her life overflowed with praise to God. She was especially thankful that she could be helpful to people, including her elderly roommate whom she helped dress every day.

"Do you want to see my room?" she asked excitedly. I agreed and was soon taken by the arm and whisked down the hall by this spry lady. "This is my little bit of heaven to go to heaven," she said contentedly, as she showed me her bed, table with her phone, T.V. and radio. She rocked rapidly back and forth in her stuffed chair. Gingerly she got up and showed me a small ceramic figurine. "I have a dog, too!" she laughed.

"How cute!" I exclaimed as I looked at the small terrier with one ear missing.

"I'll walk you back to the front entrance so you don't get lost," she volunteered.

I had never seen such a content and lively old woman. Her love for Jesus glowed in her actions. She didn't have much in material things, but her eyes were fixed on Jesus and her heavenly riches and being reunited with her loved ones. Even at her very old age, she still found ways of helping others and telling the good news that Jesus is the Savior of the world.

Prayer:
> Keep me safe, O God, for in you I take refuge. I said to the Lord, "You are my LORD; apart from you I have no good thing.". . . I will praise the LORD, who counsels me; even at night my heart instructs me. I have set the LORD always before me. Because he is at my right hand, I will not be shaken. Therefore my heart is glad and my tongue rejoices; my body also will rest secure. . .You have made known to me the path of life; you will fill me with joy in your presence, with eternal pleasures at your right hand (Psalm 16:1,2,7-9,11). Amen.

With God All Things Are Possible

Psalm 127:1
Unless the LORD builds the house, its builders labor in vain. Unless the LORD watches over the city, the watchmen stand guard in vain.

A few years ago I wrote a book from a Christian perspective for young parents about the trials and joys of raising my five children. There was a period of time before I actually got news of its acceptance by the publisher. I had sent in the manuscript and everyday ran out to my mailbox to see if it had been accepted. During that early stage of my book, there was nothing more I wanted than to have my name on the cover of a book. But God let me wait so that I would learn patience and humility.

As time passed I realized that God and his love and the love of my family were actually most important in my life. One day as I was cleaning my room, I saw the manuscript copy of my book on the closet floor. At that moment I "let go" of my book. I thought, "It was fun writing this book, but I think I'll throw it away now."

The next day God blessed me with a letter in the mail informing me of the acceptance of my book. I was thrilled! But I had learned a lesson. I decided to commit the book entirely to the Lord. Every day I prayed that I would be able to make the necessary corrections and additions which would make my book a "beautiful witness" to all who would read it, and that whenever I talked about the book, I would give all the glory to God alone. With the Lord as my partner in building the house (my book), everything went well. The illustrations came out clear and neat the first time they were duplicated. The cover looked fresh and delightful. One package of drawings I sent arrived badly damaged, but the contents were perfectly intact! The book has indeed been a blessing to many mothers, even to non-Christian mothers who have been given the book as a gift.

Each time I sit down to type a devotion, I pray first. I ask God to help the ideas flow. I ask God to give me spiritual insight to help make this book more beautiful than I could do on my own. Years ago an old ad read, "Things go better with Coke!" Someone rewrote that to make a Christian logo, "Things go better with Jesus Christ!" It is true that when we ask God to help us before we start a project, things do go better.

Everytime before I speak about parenting to a group of ladies at a church, I pray that God would give me just the right words to say to touch their hearts. Often the day before I speak, an idea will come to me. I will then add that idea as a little devotion at the beginning of my speech. Again and again ladies have come up after my speech to tell me how they were touched by my words. God alone deserves the glory for providing me with the right words. May you begin each day and each project with the Lord's blessing and guidance.

Prayer:
Dear God, with you all things are possible. Help me remember to tap your great strength and wisdom before I begin my tasks. Keep me humble, and lead me to give you all the glory for my salvation and my life. Amen.

The Good Guy Always Wins

Romans 8: 31-35, 37
If God is for us, who can be against us? He who did not spare his own Son, but gave him up for us all—how will he not also, along with him, graciously give us all things? Who will bring any charge against those whom God has chosen? It is God who justifies. Who is he that condemns? Christ Jesus, who died—more than that, who was raised to life—is at the right hand of God and is also interceding for us. Who shall separate us from the love of Christ? Shall trouble or hardship or persecution or famine or nakedness or danger or sword?...No, in all these things we are more than conquerors through him who loved us.

Sometimes I watch cartoons with my children. Almost invariably the good guy wins. One show, "Super Dave," features the hero getting run over and being shot out of a cannon, but he is always alive for the next episode. It seems silly to watch it and expend all that emotional energy wondering if he is all right, because it is only a stunt and he is always back for the next show.

It also seems silly for Christians to worry about who is going to win in real life, or whether they will live forever in heaven after they die. But it is easy to expend a lot of emotional energy worrying about such things. Why? Because the dangers we face are real. The devil is constantly trying to wear us down, getting us to surrender to doubt or temptation. And God, in his divine plan for us, may permit us to suffer illness or loss of sight, hearing or limb. Troubles in families or the work place are real, and almost every newspaper has more bad news than good news. We may grovel around in self-made prisons of guilt, wondering if we belong to God or not. If only we could see the end of the story with ourselves embraced by Jesus, safe on the heavenly shore.

But we have seen enough of the "episodes" of our life to know how it all turns out. The good guy does win! Time and again God has rescued us from trials, troubles, sicknesses and temptations. Praise be to God! Yes, the good guy does always win. We are more than conquerors through Jesus Christ. He is interceding, that is, praying for us. Is there anything God would not do to rescue us from sin and temptation? God did not spare his own Son's life. What more could he give? In life's final episode he will surely bring us safely to the heavenly shore!

At our baptism God gave us the Holy Spirit as a deposit, guaranteeing our inheritance in heaven. On the last day the Holy Spirit will give life to our mortal bodies. Romans 8:10,11 states: "But if Christ is in you. . . your spirit is alive because of righteousness. And if the Spirit of him who raised Jesus from the dead is living in you, he who raised Christ from the dead will also give life to your mortal bodies through his Spirit, who lives in you."

Prayer:
Dear God, you have given us your Holy Spirit at our baptism. Grant that we daily live in our baptismal grace and in the forgiveness of sins purchased by Jesus' blood and death on the cross, that we may live in confidence and be more than conquerors through your power. Thank you, God! Amen.

Airmail to Heaven

James 1:17
Every good and perfect gift is from above, coming down from the Father of the heavenly lights, who does not change like shifting shadows.

Have you ever received a letter from a friend? The first thing you look for is references in their letter to what you previously wrote to them. That way you know they received your letter and also that they took an interest in what you wrote.

Every night before I go to bed I "write a letter" to God. I don't really write it down. I say a prayer, but I know people who write down their prayers. The next morning when I wake up I try to recall what I prayed the night before. All that new day I look for answers to the "letter I wrote to God." I look forward to surprises from God, confident that "my letter" went through. The things that happen to me during the day are God's answer to my letter. I also read and reread his long love letter to me, his Word, and very often find it speaks right to my needs.

In my letter to God, I might pray that God would guide me to witness to someone. On one occasion, within two weeks God sent me a student in trouble, a young girl whose family was breaking up, an ill relative and other people that needed love.

At night when I have received "God's letter" to me, I can hardly wait to "write back." I remember to thank God for the specific ways he answered my "letter." I also thank him for the added surprises and blessings of the day. In this way I feel close to God, and we keep in touch.

When I pray I find that it is important to affirm God's power and ability to act and take care of me. There is a way of praying in which a person never praises God but continually begs God for help. The person praying does not thank God for the way God will act and when he will act. Rather, the person cries pitifully and hopelessly. God wants us to pray positively, praising him for how he is so faithful and loving, thanking him for how he will get us through every difficulty just as he has in the past, and giving him glory for how he will (in his time) make everything clear to us. Remember Jesus has promised, "Ask me anything in my name and I will do it." God bless your "letter writing."

Prayer:
(In the Garden)

I come to the garden alone,
While the dew is
   still on the roses,
And the voice I hear,
Falling on my ear,
The Son of God discloses.

And He walks with me,
And He talks with me,
And He tells me I am His own;
And the joy we share
   as we tarry there,
None other has ever known.

He speaks and the sound
   of His voice,
Is so sweet the birds
   hush their singing,
And the melody
That He gave to me,
Within my heart is ringing.

And He walks with me,
And He talks with me,
And He tells me I am His own;
And the joy we share
   as we tarry there,
None other has ever known.
                Amen.

Circling Things in the Christmas Catalogue

Exodus 33:14
The L<small>ORD</small> replied, "My Presence will go with you, and I will give you rest."

The time was right before Christmas. I was married with five children of my own, and my thoughts went back to my Christmases as a child. I remembered looking through the "Sears Catalogue" and my mother asking me to circle the things I wanted for Christmas. It was fun! Some of the things I circled I actually received on Christmas Eve. After dreaming about the past, I began to think in terms of what I wanted to ask God to give me this Christmas. I knew that in the realm of spiritual blessings I could circle as many things as I wanted. The sky was the limit.

There had been one thing that was not clear to me in the Bible, however, and I had wondered about it for awhile. I couldn't find the answer. Then I remembered that with God all things are possible. I trusted that God could supply the answer, and the wound from the wait could be healed. I expected the answer. An answer came and contentment flooded in on Christmas Eve. The question I had harbored for months was gone, and in its place was praise to God, the Giver of all good gifts and the Giver of rest.

Whatever spiritual need you may have, rest assured that God, in his timing, will show you the answer or lead you to someone with the answer. We have a big God and we need to think big. He is able to help us.

Jesus says in Matthew 7:7-11:

Ask and it will be given to you; seek and you will find; knock and the door will be opened to you. For everyone who asks receives; he who seeks finds; and to him who knocks, the door will be opened. Which of you, if his son asks for bread, will give him a stone? Or if he asks for a fish, will give him a snake? If you, then, though you are evil, know how to give good gifts to your children, how much more will your Father in heaven give good gifts to those who ask him!

Prayer:
Dear heavenly Father, thank you for all the good gifts you have given me. Today I pray for good gifts to fill all my spiritual needs. Please take care of those needs and help me to become more diligent in reading your Word. Amen.

The Secret of Contentment

Philippians 4:11-13
I have learned to be content whatever the circumstances. I know what it is to be in need, and I know what it is to have plenty. I have learned the secret of being content in any and every situation, whether well-fed or hungry, whether living in plenty or in want. I can do everything through him who gives me strength.

I have a wonderful Christian friend whose unbounded optimism in the face of adversity is truly admirable. She has three children. The oldest one is severely handicapped, requiring constant care. (The county provides her with caregivers for a certain number of hours a week, since she is unable to lift her son.) In spite of this burden she can be seen wheeling her son into church, her face glowing with happiness. She carves out time each week for private and group Bible Study. She drives thirty miles each day to transport her other children to a Lutheran school.

Not long ago she damaged her neck as she moved too quickly getting out of bed. The pain continued. Doctors couldn't figure out how to relieve the pain, so she lived with it. "How depressing that you have that pain all the time," I told her one day. "I bet that really bothers you."

"Oh, I praise God every day for my pain in my neck," she replied.

"You do?" I asked baffled.

"That's right. I do." She smiled one of her carefree smiles. "Our whole family has become more loving and thoughtful. My kids have to help do jobs around the house that I'm not able to do, and, because of my neck, I can't raise my voice. The children have to listen to what I say in my regular voice."

This effervescent woman with all of her problems was happier than many people who don't have problems. What was her secret of contentment? I think she trusted that in all circumstances *God would give her the necessary strength, and she praised God for working everything out for her good.*

Sometimes we do not see the immediate purpose for adversity, but we can still praise God for many things:

1. The excitement of knowing God personally and talking to him.
2. The glimpse of eternal peace we find in Holy Communion.
3. God's answers to our prayers for the conversion of others.
4. Examples of how God can turn evil into good. (Genesis 50:20)
5. The beauties of God's creation.
6. The gifts of the Holy Spirit.
7. The ability to use talents the Lord has given us.
8. The way we all support each other and fit together in the body of believers.
9. The privilege of serving Jesus by helping others.
10. The many earthly gifts God provides.
11. The comfort of God's Word.
12. The burden of sin lifted.
13. The way God again and again rescues us from the lions' mouths. (Daniel 6:22)

Prayer:

God the Father, I praise you! God the Son, I praise you! God the Holy Spirit, I praise you! You graciously supply all my needs. Dear Holy Spirit, let all people praise you so that in these dark latter days there may be those who live to praise God—each life a high doxology to Father, Son and you! Amen.

The Lost Sheep

Matthew 18:10,12-14
"See that you do not look down on one of these little ones. For I tell you that their angels in heaven always see the face of my Father in heaven. What do you think? If a man owns a hundred sheep, and one of them wanders away, will he not leave the ninety-nine on the hills and go to look for the one that wandered off? And if he finds it, I tell you the truth, he is happier about that one sheep than about the ninety-nine that did not wander off. In the same way your Father in heaven is not willing that any of these little ones should be lost."

About two years ago God put a burden on my heart to find a six-year-old boy, Jamie (not his real name). He had attended the summer Sunday school class I was teaching. Jamie lived across the street from the church, and his parents were unchurched. We were glad to have him as a visitor. He said he didn't know about Jesus, so all twenty kids in the class helped me tell him about our Savior. Jamie enthusiastically attended more summer Sunday school sessions, but he never came back when the fall sessions began.

Every month I would write a note to myself: "Visit the little boy who lives across from the church." But every month life would get so busy that I would never take time to make the visit. Every month I would scratch out the note on my calendar and add the note to the next month. Finally, by December, I thought this was getting ridiculous. I was a busy person. I had five children of my own and many church activities. I really didn't have time to make a visit to Jamie. I scratched out the note for good.

In January our Sunday School staff had a meeting. Ironically, the topic was the "Lost Sheep." God moved me to tears for this little boy, Jamie. I knew the time was "now" for me to visit him. Another teacher and I prayed together, and together we went over to his house. As we entered the house, we saw Jamie. Jamie still lived at that address. He smiled at us. We knew God had guided us there!

After talking with him and his mother, we found out that Jamie had come back to Sunday school in the fall, but he couldn't find the right room, so he had walked back home. We literally had found a lost sheep. We promised to meet Jamie at the front entrance of the church the next Sunday, and went home rejoicing.

Jesus, our Good Shepherd, seeks and finds us trapped in the wilderness of sin. He frees us from the thorns and entanglements of sin. He offers forgiveness and eternal safety within the fold. He calls us, who are his sheep, by name. John 10:27,28 says, "My sheep listen to my voice; I know them, and they follow me. I give them eternal life, and they shall never perish; no one can snatch them out of my hand."

Prayer:

Dear Jesus, my Good Shepherd, show me a lost sheep that I may find and help return to you. Be with me and give me persistence and patience in dealing with the lost. Amen.

The Open Heart

Matthew 10:19-20
"But when they arrest you, do not worry about what to say or how to say it. At that time you will be given what to say, for it will not be you speaking, but the Spirit of your Father speaking through you."

We had our house in St. Paul, Minnesota, up for sale for about two years. We could not find a buyer. "Why does God want us to stay here?" I wondered. As time went by, the answer became clear. God wanted me to be a Christian witness to my neighbors.

Vacation Bible School was fast approaching. The neighbors at the end of the block had three lovely, little blonde-haired girls. One was in preschool, one in third grade and one was a baby. A year earlier I had asked them whether they could come to VBS, and their dad had told me, "No!" But I wanted to ask them again. I knew perfectly well that I could have the door slammed in my face. But I thought, "What have I got to lose? If they slam the door on me, I'll come back home."

I prayed earnestly for a warm reception by this family. They were unchurched and I worried about the little girls not knowing Jesus. What if they would die? (One bumper sticker expresses the importance of knowing the Lord: "Don't be caught dead without Jesus.") I prayed confidently that God would open the hearts of these people and send his Holy Spirit to guide them.

As I arrived at their home, I was overwhelmed by the welcome I received. I was almost in tears as the mother warmly greeted me, and the little girls hugged and kissed me. "Sure, they'll go to VBS," the mother said in a friendly voice and then added, "I'm so glad you came, because my little girl has been asking me about Bible stories lately. I don't have all the answers."

In the following weeks I took the children to VBS, and they only missed one day due to illness. I praised God for opening the hearts of these people and for giving me the courage to visit them.

Prayer:
Dear God, prepare the way for my witness through the power of your Holy Spirit. I know that no one can say that Jesus is Lord without the Holy Spirit. Send your Holy Spirit also into my heart to strengthen me. Thank you, God! Amen.

My Pet Projects

Matthew 6:33
"But seek first his kingdom and his righteousness, and all these things will be given to you as well."

My pet projects were to do some sewing and to clean my bedroom, but the days were too busy. School had not started yet. There were kids to keep track of and feed. There was canning to be done. The more I thought about never getting time for my pet projects, the more depressed I got.

One night I realized that by not doing what *I* wanted to, I had accidentally been doing what I had long idealized a "real mother" *should* be doing. I was not too busy with my own stuff to hear the regular request, "Mom, can you read us a Bible story? We have our 'jammies' on." I would sit on the bed and read to the little boys, one, two and sometimes three stories. I would listen to their prayers, and, because I was not too busy, I had time to talk with my twelve-year-old boy.

He had just watched a scary movie on TV. I had not known the movie was on, but my son expressed lingering fear from how scary it had been. I asked my son to pray that Jesus would take the memory of the movie away. Then I read to him from 1 Timothy, chapter six: "But you, man of God, flee from all this, and pursue righteousness, godliness, faith, love, endurance and gentleness. Fight the good fight of the faith. Take hold of the eternal life to which you were called . . ." (vs. 11,12).

I added, "I bet you haven't read many of Paul's letters to the churches. They are really neat. You could read a little every night."

I handed him his Bible, and his light stayed on a long time while he read. I was glad I had not been too busy to offer help from God's Word. Helping my children grow spiritually was a lot more important than my pet projects.

God promises that, when we seek his kingdom, all the other things will be given to us as well. God later supplied me with large blocks of time for my pet projects.

Prayer:
Dear God, help me to seek your kingdom and your righteousness first. Assure me that you will supply my other needs. Thank you, God. Amen.

Opposite Day

Matthew 5:43-45

"You have heard that it was said, 'Love your neighbor and hate your enemy.' But I tell you: Love your enemies and pray for those who persecute you, that you may be sons of your Father in heaven. He causes his sun to rise on the evil and the good, and sends rain on the righteous and the unrighteous."

My kids play a game called "Opposite Day." They will say something to each other like, "Amy loves you," or "Your hair is on fire," and then tell each other that it's Opposite Day, so they mean the opposite.

Every day should be Opposite Day for us Christians. Our sinful nature wants us to sin, but with God's help we can do the opposite. The opposite of hating our enemies is loving our enemies, praying for them, even doing nice things for them. This is very hard, but remember we have the example of our Father in heaven who blesses the righteous *and* the unrighteous.

The opposite of despair is trust. When things go wrong in our life, we can trust that God will work out all things for our good.

The opposite of criticizing people is complimenting them. With God's help we can be complimentary (rather than critical) to our husbands and children.

The opposite of despising evil people is praying for them. Often the news on TV upsets me. I hear about immoral actors or actresses, nonchristian leaders, murderers, thieves, child abusers. Instead of despising these people, we can pray that Jesus would change their hearts and work a conversion as he did for Saul, who persecuted the Christians. With God's help every day can be Opposite Day!

Prayer:
Oh Holy Spirit, enter my heart and propel me beyond a mere selfish existence to give enthusiastic love and say fervent prayers for all people. Help me do your will and be a light in this drab and sinful world. Amen.

Perfect Peace

Isaiah 43:1-4
But now, this is what the Lord says—he who created you, O Jacob, he who formed you, O Israel: Fear not, for I have redeemed you; I have summoned you by name; you are mine. When you pass through the waters, I will be with you; and when you pass through the rivers, they will not sweep over you. When you walk through the fire, you will not be burned; the flames will not set you ablaze. For I am the Lord, your God, the Holy One of Israel, your Savior; I give Egypt for your ransom, Cush and Seba in your stead. Since you are precious and honored in my sight, and because I love you. . . .

On complicated, busy and harried days when my mind is diverted in three directions at once and life seems like a race, I like to remember Isaiah 26:3,4: "You will keep in perfect peace him whose mind is steadfast, because he trusts in you. Trust in the Lord forever, for the Lord, the Lord, is the Rock eternal."

All of us have had days when we may tell our children they are driving us crazy. Listen in on one of my days as a busy mother, preparing for company and trying to field questions from all directions:

"Mommy, the doggie wants more milk. Can I get some out of the refrigerator?"

"Do I have to practice piano, since we have company?"

"Mom, is the square root of the hypotenuse of an equilateral triangle equal to the sum of the two sides?"

"Mom, P. J. is cooking the plastic poodle in the toaster oven. Can you take it out before it catches on fire?"

"Mom, why can't we have soda and crackers? All the college kids downstairs at the party get some! Please, Mom?"

On very busy days I usually look for the humor in the situation and also know from experience that God always supplies peace after a "storm." I like to personalize verses from the Bible like Isaiah 43:2, "When you pass through the waters, I will be with you," to state: "When you pass through hectic days, I will be with you," "When you pass through heavy traffic, taking your daughter to ballet lessons, I will be with you," or "When you pass through knee-deep snow drifts, trying to shovel your car out of the ditch, I will be with you."

God is always present in our lives. He is our Rock, and he alone can keep us in perfect peace through Jesus Christ, our Savior. When life is a sea of trouble we can always rise above it, for we know we are safe in his love.

Prayer:
Precious Jesus, you died for me. Precious Jesus, you saved me from the yawning chasm of eternal destruction. Precious Jesus, be my Rock and keep me in perfect peace on my busy days. Amen.

The Importance of Warm Fuzzies

Philippians 2:4-7
Each of you should look not only to your own interests, but also to the interests of others. Your attitude should be the same as that of Christ Jesus: Who, being in very nature God, did not consider equality with God something to be grasped, but made himself nothing, taking the very nature of a servant....

What fun it is to receive a warm fuzzy! My husband is good at surprising me with warm fuzzies—those little things that satisfy "the need to be loved." For our fifteenth anniversary he surprised me a half month early with a yellow rose and "Happy First Anniversary" message. The next day I found a note with a box of mints tucked in my coat pocket. "Happy Second Anniversary," it read. The countdown continued until I received "Happy Fifteenth Anniversary" surprises on our actual wedding date.

Someone has guessed that we need five hugs a day to really feel good about ourselves. We all need that extra pat on the back and word of encouragement. In fact, giving out warm fuzzies is exactly what God wants us to do. We are to be imitators of Jesus, thinking of other people's interests and serving them in love. How can we imitate God's love?

The importance of warm fuzzies

1. *God's love is everlasting.* Jeremiah 31:3 tells us, "The LORD appeared to us in the past, saying: 'I have loved you with an everlasting love. . . .'" God's love does not fluctuate. We can, with God's help, love our children and others, even when they sin against us.

2. *God's love is active.* God shows his love to us by giving us many blessings. We can actively do things to show love—give hugs, compliments, little gifts, special desserts, hot chocolate, cookies, our time spent playing cards or other games with our children.

3. *God communicates his love through his spoken and written word.* We can tell our husbands and children that we love them. We can write letters and notes. Little notes of love and encouragement with "Love, Mom" on their pillows are especially good for teenagers when words at times seem awkward. We need to use written words to cheer each other. In the fall my kids and I prepared baskets of flowers with "God Loves You!" printed on construction paper daisies. The live flowers faded but the teachers who received these baskets kept the note with "God Loves You!" for a long time.

4. *God's love is personal.* God takes a personal interest in us and even numbers the hairs on our head. Through Holy Communion God assures us individually of his great love. We can take a personal interest in our family members by remembering them with birthday and baptism day cakes. We can show interest in their projects and hobbies, and listen to them as God constantly listens to us.

5. *God's love goes before us.* God anticipates our needs. In Isaiah 65:24 the Lord God promises, "Before

they call I will answer; while they are still speaking I will hear." God so carefully plans our experiences in life that we may rejoice in his love. We cannot see the future, but we can imitate God by anticipating needs—the afternoon snack, the hot cocoa ready when the kids come in from sledding, the hot meal for the hungry husband coming home from work, the ironed dress for a party, the special outing with mom to get a haircut.

6. *God's love is forgiving.* Even on the cross Jesus forgave people. No one has nailed us to a cross, and yet sometimes we arbitrarily set up rules for "the last straw!" We fail to forgive as much as God has forgiven us. With God's help we can forgive again and again.

7. *God's love pleads for us.* God prays for us. Jesus told Peter in Luke 22:32, "But I have prayed for you, Simon, that your faith may not fail." In Romans 8:26 we find that the Holy Spirit intercedes for us. Some mothers use Ephesians 3 below as a prayer for their children. May God give you joy, as you try to imitate his love!

Prayer:
For this reason I kneel before the Father, from whom his whole family in heaven and on earth derives its name. I pray that out of his glorious riches he may strengthen you with power through his Spirit in your inner being, so that Christ may dwell in your hearts through faith. And I pray that you, being rooted and established in love, may have power, together with all the saints, to grasp how wide and long and high and deep is the love of Christ, and to know this love that surpasses knowledge—that you may be filled to the measure of all the fullness of God (Ephesians 3:14-19). Amen.

Living on the Mountain Top

Matthew 17:1-8
After six days Jesus took with him Peter, James and John the brother of James, and led them up a high mountain by themselves. There he was transfigured before them. His face shone like the sun, and his clothes became as white as the light. Just then there appeared before them Moses and Elijah talking with Jesus.

Peter said to Jesus, "Lord it is good for us to be here. If you wish, I will put up three shelters—one for you, one for Moses and one for Elijah."

While he was still speaking, a bright cloud enveloped them, and a voice from the cloud said, "This is my Son, whom I love; with him I am well pleased. Listen to him!"

When the disciples heard this, they fell face down to the ground, terrified. But Jesus came and touched them. "Get up," he said. "Don't be afraid." When they looked up they saw no one except Jesus.

My favorite place to get away from the busy life I lead in St. Paul, Minnesota, is the farm. It is not just any farm, but the best farm on earth, the place where I spent my carefree childhood days, the beautiful place with fresh air and wide open spaces, the loving place where I was cared for so well the first seventeen years of my life.

My folks and my brother still live on the farm and it is still the beautiful haven it always was—a place to relax and refresh and laugh and enjoy life, a place to savor wonderfully prepared food and sink deeply into feather pillows at night.

The family farm is my "mountain top." You can imagine that I would not be in a hurry to leave such a wonderful place, and recently those were my exact sentiments. The kids were off from school on Monday, so I planned to stay at the farm the whole weekend. But Sunday afternoon I received a call from a daycare center in St. Paul that needed a preschool teacher for Monday.

I was feeling blue as I drove through ever increasing traffic to the big, noisy city. Why couldn't I stay in the haven of love and warmth on the farm? Why did I have to go back to the smog and daily grind of the city?

The answer was clearly shown to me by God the next day. The ocean of love and security I had received was meant to be shared. The rich feeding in God's Word I had experienced through family devotions, Lutheran school and college was meant to be shared with people who lived on the "plain." That Monday God led me down the mountain to see the needs of the people below. He showed me that there can be joy also on the plain, because he is there too.

At the daycare, I met Lori (not her real name). I asked her what church she went to, and she said she never joined a church because her parents never took her. But when she got married she planned to join one. Later that afternoon we had time to talk while the kids took naps (an hour and a half!). "When you decide to join a church," I ventured, "be certain that it's one that teaches that Jesus is God and Savior, and that the only way of salvation is through his death for our sins."

We talked and talked. She had many questions about what Christians believe. The best part of the story is that God had prepared her heart to receive the

Gospel. As we parted that day, I handed her a small devotional booklet. She was openly appreciative to receive it. I left the center with my feet in the clouds. There certainly was much joy on the plain, too, sharing the vast expanse of God's love.

I thought of hymn #507 of The Lutheran Hymnal:

Spread, oh, spread thou mighty Word,
Spread the kingdom of the Lord,
Wheresoe'er His breath has given
Life to beings meant for heaven.

Lord of Harvest let there be
Joy and strength to work for Thee
Till the nations far and near
See Thy light and learn Thy fear.
(vs 1,6)

Prayer:
Lord, help me lead people on the "plain" to know you so that they may experience mountain-top joy too. Amen.

Evelyn's Shining Light

James 5:16-18
The prayer of a righteous man is powerful and effective.
Elijah was a man just like us. He prayed earnestly that it would not rain, and it did not rain on the land for three and a half years. Again he prayed, and the heavens gave rain, and the earth produced its crops.

I have a sixtyish friend named Evelyn (not her real name), who is a shining light for Jesus. Her prayer life attests to God's faithfulness in answering our prayers. Evelyn regularly prayed for an opportunity to witness to someone.

One day on the bus home from work she sat by a young man who was smoking. After talking to him for a while, she found out that his despair in trying to find his real mother had led him to drugs. After being in a "detox" center, he turned to heavy smoking.

Every day she would meet him on the bus and in her own quiet way, in small amounts, Evelyn would witness to him of his Savior, Jesus, who loved him. Every day the man would listen to her speak. One day when she met him on the bus, he was bubbling over with news. He had found his mother, quit smoking and was telling others how wonderful he felt becoming a Christian. Evelyn's prayer for someone to witness to was definitely answered.

Evelyn's story of answered prayer continues. One of the people visiting the office where she worked noticed the Christian pin she was wearing. The man mentioned that he was a Muslim married to a Christian woman. His wife wanted him to convert to Christianity, but he was finding it very hard. Evelyn said that she would pray for him. Several months later he came into the office, all smiles. He had become a Christian. He wanted Evelyn to pray for his parents so that they, too, would become Christians.

Evelyn asked God to lead her to people to witness to, and he did. We must remember that the power did not lie in Evelyn because she was a wonderful Christian. The power always lies in God. His Holy Spirit works powerfully in the hearts of people to change them. But God uses people like Evelyn and you and me to tell people quietly in our own words how God loves them.

Prayer:
Dear Jesus, I want to be a shining light for you to point people to heaven. Please give me the opportunity to witness to someone and give me the words to say. Thank you, Jesus. Amen.

Make My Life an Alleluia!

God's Mighty Acts

Psalm 145: 1-12
I will exalt you, my God the King; I will praise your name for ever and ever. Every day I will praise you and extol your name for ever and ever.

*Great is the L*ORD *and most worthy of praise; his greatness no one can fathom. One generation will commend your works to another; they will tell of your mighty acts. They will speak of the glorious splendor of your majesty, and I will meditate on your wonderful works. They will tell of the power of your awesome works, and I will proclaim your great deeds. They will celebrate your abundant goodness and joyfully sing of your righteousness.*

*The L*ORD *is gracious and compassionate, slow to anger and rich in love. The L*ORD *is good to all, he has compassion on all he has made. All you have made will praise you, O L*ORD*; your saints will extol you. They will tell of the glory of your kingdom and speak of your might, so that all men may know of your mighty acts and the glorious splendor of your kingdom.*

Two years ago our eight year old son, Micah, was stricken with a 102 degree fever. A dose of Tylenol, given at bedtime, only seemed to elevate the fever. By midnight he had become even hotter and delirious.

When the fever did not subside after three days, we knew it wasn't a simple flu bug. We did what any concerned parent would do. We took him to the doctor, trusting that the doctor would give him medicine, and that would take care of it. But the penicillin prescribed by the doctor took no effect even after three days use.

By this time we were really worried. Micah's energy level and appetite decreased dramatically. Our once active boy lay on the couch and had no desire for food. Perhaps we had put too much trust in doctors. God was leading us to grow in patience, endurance and persistence in prayer.

No improvement was in sight. Every morning Micah's temperature was 99 or 100 degrees and every afternoon it rose to 102 degrees. This continued for twelve days. Finally I put Micah on our prayer chain at church. About that same time Micah's teacher suggested that sometimes European doctors might know more about strange penicillin resistant diseases.

With earnest prayer my husband took Micah in to see a British doctor. She was able to diagnose the problem quickly as viral pneumonia in both lungs! After a couple of doses of a stronger medicine, erythromycin, Micah was beginning to perk up. We praised God for every step of his improvement.

The next day, Sunday, was Micah's sister's confirmation. It was such a joy to see Micah sit up at the table and join us in the meal. Even though he ate very little, we thanked God for giving Micah his health.

We have told many people about God's mighty act of healing Micah. Through the bitter time of testing, we learned to rely on God and also to sympathize with other parents whose children had similar illnesses at the time.

When God brings us through sickness or hard times, he wants us to tell others about his mighty acts. He wants us to realize our dependency on him so that he receives all the glory. May God help us to remember this.

Prayer:
Dear Jesus, you are the Great Physician of body and soul. Look with compassion on the sick and heal them if it is your will. Open my mouth to speak of your mighty acts. Amen.

Pray About Everything

Philippians 4:6
Do not be anxious about anything, but in everything, by prayer and petition, with thanksgiving, present your requests to God.

It is an exciting time of life when your oldest child goes on her first date. But when the young couple rides away in a car, you realize that the date is completely out of your hands. Nevertheless, wherever your son or daughter may be, you know that they are always in God's hands, and that they are as close as a prayer.

I have prayed for my daughter many times throughout her high school years. God has always heard my prayers and blessed her. It may seem frivolous to pray about little things like a date or a misunderstanding between friends, but God cares about every detail in our lives and our children's lives. It is comforting to know that we can cast all of our cares on him because he cares for us.

A lady was given an assignment to make "PRAY" signs and attach them all over the house in every room as a reminder to pray about everything. After a week she noticed that she was much more carefree, committing everything to God in prayer.

Along with remembering to pray, we must remember that with God all things are possible. We can also take big things to God in prayer. Think of the impossible odds David faced fighting the giant, Goliath. Do you have Goliaths in your own life? Do huge problems threaten you, like your teenager's mutiny, financial problems, the midwinter blahs, or a habit of using bad language? What about parent-teenager arguments? Many times when our family's parent-teenager relationship seemed at a deadlock, I have prayed for a solution and almost miraculously reconciliation has occurred.

What about financial problems? God can supply the jobs we need to meet our daily needs. Last fall, my friend, Kay, prayed for me to find a job since we really needed some extra income for our Lutheran high school. Within the week, I had four jobs, one at a montessori preschool, one at a Lutheran school part-time, one as a waitress on weekends, and one assisting my son on his new paper route.

The mid-winter blahs are a tricky, problem because we don't realize they are there until we have been depressed for some time. The long winter, the cloudy sky and the daily grind at work, all contribute to that feeling. The best remedy I found this winter was a midweek tea and service of prayer and praise with our women's group at church. First, we enjoyed hot cider, delicious bars and Christian fellowship. Then we committed our worries to God in a service of prayer and song. The service was highlighted with the celebration of Holy Communion. Even in the dull, drab mid-winter season, Christ assured us all intimately of his presence with us. "The Lord is with you. Go in peace," echoed in our ears as we left the church.

What about bad habits? We know the more we try to overcome them on our own, the worse they become. We need God's supernatural power to overcome them. We can pray for the Holy Spirit to guide our thoughts so that the bad words will not come out. We can pray for the gift of patience from the Holy Spirit. Finally we can take time to immerse our minds in God's Word through group and private Bible study.

"Finally, brothers, whatever is true, whatever is noble, whatever is right, whatever is pure, whatever is lovely, whatever is admirable—if anything is excellent or praiseworthy—think about such things" (Philippians 4:8).

Prayer:
Dear Jesus, increase my trust in you. Take all my worries and cares. In your own time, Jesus, help me work through all my problems. Lead me to praise you now and forever. Amen.

Motivation for Prayer

Daniel 6:25-27
Then King Darius wrote to all the peoples, nations and men of every language throughout the land:
"May you prosper greatly!
"I issue a decree that in every part of my kingdom people must fear and reverence the God of Daniel.
"For he is the living God and he endures forever; his kingdom will not be destroyed, his dominion will never end. He rescues and he saves; he performs signs and wonders in the heavens and on the earth. He has rescued Daniel from the power of the lions."

One hot summer evening I was trying arduously to curtail a few of my kids' loud and boisterous conversations at the dinner table so that I could read the devotion. We finally had the devotion, but what a chore to get them settled.

After dinner, I cleared the dishes and went up to change the beds. I couldn't figure out why our otherwise healthy dog, Zipper, was vomiting on the bedroom carpet. I zoomed down to the kitchen to get some paper towels. I took one look at the kitchen floor and screamed. "Zipper ate the ant poison!" I blurted out hysterically.

All of the children quickly gathered around. To kill the ants, I had put some sweetened condensed milk on a piece of cardboard and laced it with "Terro Ant Killer." Zipper licked it clean! It has arsenic in it. It says, "**Keep away from children and pets.**" Zipper could die!

Two of my older children dialed the emergency veterinary service and poison control.

"Put a teaspoon of salt in the back of the dogs

soon the dog should be vomiting again. "However, if the dog persists in vomiting, it could mean possible death from loss of body fluids within two hours."

My son had already gotten the salt out of the cupboard, and within seconds we administered the correct dose. The children had all been listening to the seriousness of the conversation. "Now, we're going to pray," I said quickly. It was very quiet. "Dear God, make Zipper better. Amen."

I could tell that the full attention of each child was directed to that prayer. No one moved a muscle. At that moment they had real motivation for prayer.

For that night the dog was sickly, but made a quick recovery the next day.

What things motivate people to pray? Isn't it often sickness or death of a loved one? Often a tragic turn of events, such as the loss of a job, brings people to their knees. If a loved one is dying, usually that is a chief motivator. When life is uneventful, however, meditating on Christ's death can motivate us to pray. Christ died a horrible, painful death on the cross. There is a church called "Holy Cross Lutheran Church." The cross is not the holy object. But Christ, who is pure and holy, was nailed to an ugly cross to bear the sins of all people. The love of Jesus to endure a death like that for us motivates us to thank him. Finally, thinking beyond his death to his powerful, victorious resurrection motivates us to add praises.

Prayer:
Dear God, thank you for rescuing me again and again from the power of the lions in my life. Thanks most of all for rescuing me from the worst lions: sin, death and the devil. Keep me mindful of my salvation and fervent in prayer. Amen.

The Wonderful Winter Wonderland

James 1:17
Every good and perfect gift is from above, coming down from the Father of the heavenly lights, who does not change like shifting shadows.

I was awakened in the morning by the blaring sound of radios announcing school closings. Today would be the first snow day of the school year. Rain and freezing temperatures the night before left glacier-like sheets of ice on our driveway and the road. The shouts rang out from our troops: "No school!"

The day before, I had coveted time for myself on the computer, but now the beauty of the outdoors beckoned me. Downy flakes as big as feathers floated down, and lovely snow-laden branches were outlined in white against the blue sky.

I made a hot lunch for my five children. What a blessing to have them all home and eating lunch together, especially since the oldest was usually busy with high school sports and social events. As we rolled snowballs in the backyard and worked to make a huge snow jump for the sled, my heart filled with thankfulness to God for this day we had to spend together. I also enjoyed the time in the kitchen making special pies (cherry, chocolate and lemon meringue) for my family to enjoy.

God the Father has filled our lives with many good and perfect gifts, the best being the gift of his only Son as our Savior. With our eternity secure, we can thoroughly enjoy all of the good things he sends our way, knowing that he is there with us to bless our days and increase our joy.

Truly we have a "Beautiful Savior":

Beautiful Savior, King of creation
Son of God and Son of Man!
Truly I'd love Thee,
Truly I'd serve Thee,
Light of my soul, my Joy, my Crown.

Fair are the meadows,
Fair are the woodlands,
Robed in flowers of blooming spring;
Jesus is fairer,
Jesus is purer;
He makes our sorrowing spirit sing.

Prayer:
Dear Heavenly Father, thank you for the good gifts you give us—food, clothes, homes, families, friends, the beauty of nature. We praise you especially for the gift of your Son to give us eternal life. Bless our days. In Jesus' name. Amen.

Things that Go "Bump" in the Night

Psalm 91:1-6,14,15
He who dwells in the shelter of the Most High will rest in the shadow of the Almighty. I will say of the LORD, "He is my refuge and my fortress, my God, in whom I trust."

Surely he will save you from the fowler's snare and from the deadly pestilence. He will cover you with his feathers, and under his wings you will find refuge; his faithfulness will be your shield and rampart. You will not fear the terror of night, nor the arrow that flies by day, nor the pestilence that stalks in the darkness, nor the plague that destroys at midday.

"Because he loves me," says the LORD, "I will rescue him; I will protect him, for he acknowledges my name. He will call upon me, and I will answer him; I will be with him in trouble, I will deliver him and honor him."

I am a night owl. I love to stay up at night and do some writing or sewing. One night I was up until 2:30 A.M. washing our large downstairs floor. I reasoned that it was the only time the kids are off it, but as I hung up my rubber gloves and went to the kitchen to turn off the lights, I wondered about the wisdom of staying up late.

There is a deadly silence in the house when everyone is asleep. I begin to hear sounds I don't hear during the daytime—perhaps a cat in the garbage can outside, the clanking of the heat registers. Sometimes, too, I think I see shadows, as fear takes over. The darkness seems to close in, as one by one I dim the lights. I remember Ephesians 6:12: "For our struggle is not against flesh and blood, but against. . .the spiritual forces of evil in the heavenly realms."

Just as fear seems to have cornered me, I break out in a lusty chorus of the Easter hymn, "Christ the Lord is Risen Today, Alleluia!" The fears leave. On the first Easter, Christ conquered the devil and all his might. We need only to claim that victory and we can sleep in peace. God is our protector. As we go to sleep we can pray that God send angels to stand around the house and around each bed.

Once, our family took a ten-day vacation. When we returned home, the back door was standing half open. Evidently we had closed the door when we left, but the latch had not caught. Carefully my husband and oldest son explored every room for evidence of a prowler. Finding none, they beckoned us to come in from the car. Everything was perfectly intact, including all of our blank checks! God's protection was complete while we were gone, in spite of the unlatched door.

Prayer:
God the Father, thank you for protecting me from the evil one. Keep me in your protection always. Thank you! Amen.